PLAYTRAINING YOUR DOG

PLAYTRAINING YOUR DOG

Patricia Gail Burnham

Photographs by
Dusty Wasserman

ST. MARTIN'S PRESS
New York

Library of Congress Cataloging in Publication Data
Burnham, Patricia Gail.
    Playtraining your dog.
    1. Dogs—Training. I. Title.
SF431.B94 636.7'08'87 80-14547
ISBN 0-312-61689-9

Designed by Nancy Dale Muldoon

Photo Credits
Dusty Wasserman
p. 150, photo by Joan Ludwig.
pp. 23, 239, photos by Rich Bergman.

1.

From left to right: Sunny-Field Champion California Sunshine Traveler, Utility Dog; Tiger-Champion and Field Champion Midnight Shadow Traveler, Utility Dog, Tracker; Trip-Champion Clairidge Light Fantastic; Companion Dog Excellent Kitty Hawk-Champion Clairidge Kitty Hawk, Companion Dog. (Photo by Joan Ludwig)

FOR THE DOGS,
without whom there would have been no book.

FOR DUSTY,
without whom there would have been no photographs.

AND FOR MY PARENTS,
without whom there would have been no author.

"KINDNESS IS POWER"

John S. Rarey, nineteenth-century horse tamer

CONTENTS

THE HEART OF PLAYTRAINING
How to Create the Dog that You Want

Getting What You Want

Dog owners are like other people. They want what they want when they want it. They expect from their dogs everyday doglike devotion, routine heroics, and movie-style intelligence. All dogs do not come naturally equipped with these qualities. They have to be developed. You can create the nearly perfect companion dog but doing so requires thought.

I will tell you an important truth right at the beginning: You will receive back from the dog only what you put into him. Dogs that are loved love in return. Dogs that are educated develop their minds. Dogs that are communicated with learn to communicate with their owners. Dogs that are respected achieve self-respect and confidence. A dog in close contact with a person will become what the person wishes, *if the owner knows enough about dogs to create the dog he wants*. It is sad to see well-intentioned owners invest months and years of effort in training dogs, only to create monsters of their own design. A person gets the dog that he deserves. This book is a guide to raising the quality of both your dog and your dog-owner relationship.

1

Why the Obedience Exercises?

The exercises that we use in the book are the American Kennel Club exercises for the three obedience classes: Novice, Open, and Utility. These are used mainly for convenience because they are widely known and standardized. The obedience exercises are not the only ones that can be taught. The dog could just as well be learning gun-dog work, livestock handling, show ring routines, or protection procedures. It is the learning itself that matters, not what is being learned.

Problem Training

Most of the dogs enrolled in obedience classes are not there to be trained for trial competition. Neither are they there to be helped in rounding out their personalities. They are in class because the owner has discovered that he has a problem on the other end of the leash. Since he is more conscientious than the average dog owner (the average dog owner with a problem sends the dog to the animal shelter), the trainer-owner resorts to obedience training in an attempt to correct the problem. What he finds at many obedience classes is a series of corrections and punishments intended to redesign the dog's behavior. In most cases, these corrections were specifically designed for use on problem dogs. Almost always they were patterned on the knowledge of dog training gained from the training of defense and police dogs. The majority of the money devoted to the training of dogs has been supplied by the government for work in these two areas. Many professional trainers spent a good deal of their time being paid by the only available large customer for their services, and training dogs for the armed forces. This creates a problem. In a defense training program large numbers of dogs have to be trained in the shortest possible time. There is a minority of dogs that love to be corrected. They are masochists. The more they are corrected, the more they love their owners and the better they work. If quite a few of the more normal dogs wash out under the training pressure, replacements are always available. Before the program even starts, the shy and less assertive dogs are culled. Training methods developed to train tough, aggressive dogs in minimum amounts of time are not going to work well on most dogs.

Fortunately, there is an alternative for the person who is not planning to train attack dogs and who has an aversion to the violence that conventional methods inflict on both the bodies and, more importantly, the minds of the dogs.

Play

Play is a word for which most of the dictionary definitions are unsatisfactory. The closest thing to an acceptable Webster definition is "the spontaneous activity of children"; yet this immediately raises the question of why it is a child's activity. Are adults not allowed to play? In our society adults have something called recreation instead of play, and they work at recreation with grim determination. Whether it consists of long-distance motor trips or mountain-climbing, recreation can be tiring and painful. Having grown up, we have to work for our play. The reason that we can make do without a good official definition of play is that each adult has sufficient experience from his childhood to know what play is in practice if not in theory. Each also has a need to play in a world where adults are expected to have outgrown that need. This produces tension and from it we get a host of play rip-off words. There are the friendly ones that recognize the wistful will to play such as play ball, word play, and playful. And then there are the play repression words that indicate irresponsibility and immaturity, such as playboys, play around, and play the field. What all these words have in common is that none of them describes actual play. I finally did find a good definition of play by relying on a person for it instead of a dictionary. He suggested that "play is a spontaneous activity that produces pleasure, creative satisfaction, and self-fulfillment. Play often involves an agreed-on structure context with rules, setting, beginning and outcome agreed upon by the participants." You will note that nothing is said about the age of the players.

Many adults have not played in so long that they have forgotten how to do it. Most have an unmet need to play and only limited or unsatisfactory access to socially acceptable ways of doing so. The most common acceptable way of achieving play for an adult is to have children, and to play with them and their toys. This leads to the perennial Christmas jokes about the children who cannot get near their train sets or other toys because their dad is playing with them. Still, having children is a considerable investment for the privilege of being allowed to engage in play. There are more readily available, less expensive, playmates for us in the form of pets. Dogs, for instance, are not picky. They will play with whatever creature they find themselves living with, whether that is another dog, a cat, or a person.

Play is an activity in which both players are acting totally in the present. Why does throwing a stick for a dog to retrieve please the owner and engross his attention? It is a rudimentary game of catch. Why is it fun to run away from a dog that you know from long experience is going to run you down and smile as he passes? It is the essential game of tag, and the moment the dog goes by—"Tag, You're It"—is a triumph and delight for both participants. Tug of war, and keep away, and just plain wrestling are also high on a dog's list of play skills. Play with a young puppy and you will find it wrestling with your puppy-sized hand to the pleasure of all concerned.

Now we come to the curious part. Many people maintain an adult-to-adult relationship with their dogs. They seem unable to play with their dogs. The dogs raised in this type of environment lose their play skills. Why should we not play with dogs? They are available and eager to play. If the owner can unbend enough to participate, he will find that his own desire to play is still alive beneath his repression of it.

The Alternative—Playtraining

What is the basis of playtraining? The first requirement for any type of training is motivation. Dogs desire their owner's company and attention above all else. In order to receive human contact and praise, most dogs will cheerfully endure what appears to them to be a lot of nonsense rules. For instance, it really does not make much sense to the dog to have to jump over a hurdle that is only five feet wide when it is much easier to go around the obstacle. However, once they learn what is expected, the dogs humor us. They play the

The Heart of Playtraining

How to Create the Dog that You Want

game by our rules. All puppies, and those adult dogs that have not been too discouraged, want to play. They are perfectly willing to play with their two-footed friends. Dog games, whether with a person or another dog, are structured. The games have carefully respected rules. The handler can make obedience a series of games, which the dog will be happy to play, by gradually creating guidelines to shape the games into the obedience exercises. Does this sound like a lot of work? It had better not be or the dog will decide not to play. Conventional obedience is work. Playtraining is fun for both the dog and owner. Are you accustomed to conventional methods, and do you doubt that playtraining can work? A series of pictures is worth more than all the words that could be used.

The Trip Flip

The photo sequence shows a greyhound named Trip performing the obedience finish by an optional and acceptable method called the flip. All the obedience finish requires is that, on a single command, the dog move from the position in Figure 2 to the heel position in Figure 7. How the dog

While waiting for her cue, Trip's total attention is fixed on her handler. Note the eye contact between the two.

On the word "Heel" she throws herself straight up and to the handler's left. At the highest point in the leap, she is in proper heel position except that she is four feet too high and facing 180 degrees

manages this is left up to the dog and handler. In the conventional finish the dog simply gets up, walks a three-quarter circle around the handler, and sits at heel. In the military finish the dog walks past the handler's left side and then turns around and sits. In the swing finish the dog swings its hindquarters in a counterclockwise half-circle while doing a small pivot in place with its front feet, to get from a position facing the handler to one sitting next to her. The flip finish is a swing finish done entirely in the air. The flip finish was chosen to illustrate this section because it is an outstanding example of an obedience that cannot be taught by the use of

in the wrong direction. She then swings her head and tail to the side and rotates her body. As she falls, she continues to turn until she lands in the heel position.

negative corrections. No dog can be *made* to do a flip finish. Trip has no idea that it is an obedience exercise. She thinks that it is a game, and one of her favorite games at that. She did at least twenty flips for the photo session, and each one was a little higher and more enthusiastic than the last.

Obedience does not have to be like an army basic training camp, where the dog is the recruit and the trainer is the drill instructor. It does not have to be work. It can be play with a few rules to shape the game gently into an obedience exercise. The play system takes longer to teach than the army camp method, but I do not mind the extra time because it is

Does it look as if Trip and her handler are having fun? Why should obedience be work, or be dull? Let's make it dog play.

fun. The play method takes longer only in terms of elapsed months for teaching a dog all the exercises. It actually takes a minimum of training time, because the training sessions are very short. In the middle of a walk in the park we do a minute of heeling, three retrieves, and a recall and then go on with the walk. With conventional methods we were training twenty to forty minutes a day, five days a week.

Intelligent dogs learn exercises quickly. They also learn that long training sessions are a bore, and then the handler is in trouble. It is possible to show and complete titles on a dog that does not willingly cooperate with the handler, but it is not enjoyable. If it is not enjoyable, then why bother doing it? The objective of playtraining is to make living, training, and showing fun for both the dog and owner. How do you start playtraining? First you learn to talk to your dog.

Dog Talk—The First Incentive

Do you chat casually with your dog in private? Are you embarrassed to be heard talking to it in public? Many dog owners are. However, the more a dog is talked to, the more responsive it becomes to verbal control. The handler's general conversation helps the dog develop skill in reading people's moods from voice patterns. It will learn often-repeated phrases and sentences. There is an obedience myth that commands should consist of a single short word. Presumably the dog is too stupid to remember more than one word. The talked-to dog has no trouble expanding his vocabulary to include such things as: "Let's go home and have dinner," "Get your feet off the gearshift" (Tiger has a penchant for shifting the car from fourth to third on the freeway), or "Go into the kitchen and lie down." What does all this have to do with formal obedience? It produces a dog that pays attention to what is said, draws correct conclusions from what it is told, and acts accordingly. The desired goal is a dog that can be *talked* through the exercises. This means the substitution of verbal control, which you always have, for leash control. Eventually, grimacing and saying "Ick" or "Pay attention" can take the place of collar corrections. The leash is an invaluable training aid, but only one exercise is done on leash in competition.

Correcting a dog in the ring, even between exercises, is not permitted. Talking to the dog between the exercises is allowed, and I highly recommend it.

One would think that it would be easy to get novice trainers to talk to their dogs. It is incredibly difficult. They cannot think of anything to say after the first two sentences. Then they become self-conscious and lapse into silence. They require constant reminders and encouragement to continue talking until they finally invent a dog-talk pattern of their own, which is a repetitive monologue that maintains contact with the animal. What is said does not matter. The sound of the voice is what counts. Horse fanciers are much better at this than are dog folk, because horses require constant verbal reassurance to avoid being startled and to keep their owner safe from a quick kick. The only dog person whom I have ever heard begin talking to a dog at the first suggestion and continue without lapses or interruptions was a professional breed handler. I had never heard breed handlers use dog talk and thought that they considered it somehow beneath them, but he had obviously developed the skill for his own training purposes. Everyone creates his own repetitive phrases for the monologue. A typical series goes something like this: "Hi, dog. Would you like to play? Would you like to play the game? O.K. Sit. What is that? Sit straight. Good girl, that was pretty, now heel. Pay attention now, watch the turn. Oops. Let's try that again. Watch it now, good girl. That was better. How is the pupzer; are you having fun?" The monologue runs on and on. I only reproduce it to show that whatever you decide to say to your dog will not be any sillier than what I say, and there is no reason to feel self-conscious about it. The dog on the receiving end of this commentary has no need to worry about how he or she is doing. The dog has constant reassurance at every point in the exercise of just how pleased the owner is.

Once the dog is trained and close to being ready to show, short breaks are introduced in the monologue. They are gradually widened until the dog will forgive an occasional silent performance of each exercise. The dog is still talked to between exercises, and at least one-third of ring time is spent between exercises. The dog is also still talked to during practice sessions. Dogs, like children, friends, and lovers, blossom under steady praise and encouragement. They cannot receive too much appreciation. Even really rotten working dogs do not get any better if they are told how bad they are. If you can bite your tongue and praise the faintest good points in a performance; or if you can praise a performance that really has no good points, you can gradually restore enough self-confidence to the dog to enable him to work better the next time. It goes against the grain at first to praise a dog that is working poorly, but it is effective. It has a much more beneficial effect on the dog's performance than correcting a dog that is already resisting working.

When a dog is working exceptionally well, there is a temptation to assume that he does not need to be praised. If you stop the praise, eventually the dog will stop working well. Why should it continue to excel for someone who it feels is unappreciative?

The Thinking Trainer

Once the dog is verbally responsive, it is time to consider training techniques. One widespread fallacy is that there is one best way to teach a dog a particular exercise. *There are as many ways to teach a dog a given exercise as you can find and try*. Do not get locked into a method that is not working for your particular dog. Class trainers tend to be revered authority figures. Nevertheless, if a class trainer insists that only a particular method will work, he is displaying his own ignorance. Resist the suggestion and find a method that will work for you and your dog. Reject any methods that do not work and keep thinking of new ones to try. The secret here is to keep thinking. Observe the dog's reaction to a technique. If it was a failure, why did the dog not respond to it? If it succeeded, what were its positive qualities? What did the dog think of it? The ability to see the procedure from a dog's-eye view is one of the most valuable abilities a trainer can have.

Many failures are due to a lack of understanding. The owner tries to teach one thing, but the dog, seeing it from a different point of view, learns something quite different. Training of a sort has taken place, but the intended lesson was not taught. The classic examples of this type of failure are the many dogs who are carefully taught *not* to be house-trained. These dogs usually do not have a great deal of dog-owner contact. The owner goes off to work and the dog feels ignored. One day he learns that by being the reverse of housebroken he can attract attention. It is adverse attention, but that does not matter. To the isolated dog, any attention is desirable. So the dog keeps making intentional mistakes to ask for attention and the owner keeps rewarding him with punishment, which is a form of attention. The owner is completely unable to understand why the punishment does not train the dog, because he does not realize that this is what the dog is seeking. What we then have is a dog that has trained its owner to react in a lively manner whenever the dog gives the signal—the signal being little piles and puddles in the house. To repeat, training has taken place, but, at least from the owner's point of view, the desired response was not taught. In order to train a dog and produce the best possible response, the trainer has to work on improving his own skills and knowledge.

Anxiety Faults

A handler related her difficulties with a dog that was a chronic whiner in the long downs. She described every possible form of punishment that could be used for whining and said that none of them had worked. Why had punishment not worked? Because whining is an anxiety fault. The dog starts out by being nervous, so he whines. He is then punished for whining, which confirms his initial belief that something awful is about to happen to him. Now even more nervous, the dog whines some more. If someone put me on a sit stay command and did to me the things the lady had tried on her dog, I would do some whining myself. Active punishment of an anxiety fault like whining or sniffing intensifies the problem. The more the dog is punished, the more compulsive he becomes.

In starting with one untrained dog that was already a whiner, I have varied the exercises to take his mind off the whine. We worked at building his confidence, and, aside from occasionally telling him mildly that whining was not polite, ignored it. He proved to be an eager learner. By the end of three weeks he realized that obedience was fun and he stopped whining, except while waiting impatiently for his turn to work. He could easily have been turned into a chronic ring whiner with a little punishment. You will get from a dog (or for that matter from a person) whatever behavior you pay attention to. They never forget the attention-getters. For this reason it is a good idea not to pay much attention to anything that you do not want to see a lot more of in the future.

When Kitty Hawk was ready to show in Novice class, she had one problem. She was a compulsive sniffer and somewhat insecure. I decided to let her take the possible penalties rather than reduce her already insignificant self-confidence by trying to end the sniffing. The first time shown she did her expected forty-five-second-long sniff during the down. At each successive show the elapsed sniff time grew shorter and shorter. Before she was through showing, she was all sniffed out and gave it up as boring. Along the way none of her judges took points off for the sniffing.

The opposite of praise is not punishment. Praise and punishment are both forms of attention, and dogs crave attention. (So do people large and small.) The opposite of being praised is to be ignored.

You praise the good to get more of it. You ignore the bad so that it will disappear. It disappears because it doesn't get any attention.

The Trainer's Goal

The usual belief is that training is something that is done to the dog—that the ultimate goal of a trainer is a well-trained dog as a finished product. Actually, the well or poorly trained dog is an incidental product of the training process. The ultimate goal of training is the education and skill development of the trainer, a process that never ends. That is why trainers can stay with the sport for thirty or fifty years. The trainer's hope is that each dog he trains will increase his abilities, and that as a result each succeeding dog will be better than the one that preceded it. There is a saying that a trainer always ruins his first dog. This is not literally true. Many first dogs are very successful. But the saying is always true from the trainer's point of view. Looking back over his work with that first dog, he can see, with the knowledge gained from that dog, what the mistakes were. He can see what could have been done, no matter how good the dog is, to have made it better. He can then apply that knowledge to the next dog.

This would be a simple refining process leading quickly to perfection, except for the catch. The catch is that the next dog is a different individual that has its own behavior patterns and characteristics. So the learning process begins again for both dog and handler. The dogs may be learning the same exercises, but the handler should be learning something new each time. The hope is that each succeeding dog will have a greater opportunity to work to the top of its ability than its predecessor did. Sometimes there are failures, which can teach even more than the successes. It is just as essential to know which methods to avoid as it is to know the helpful ones.

While showing a pair of dogs for their Open titles, I used to enter one in Open A and the other in Open B to be sure they would be separated for the group exercise* As I went from the Open A group exercises to those in Open B, an interesting contrast in the handlers became apparent. What handlers do during the out-of-sight sits and downs is talk. The opening question in the Open A group is, "Who is still passing—who has passed the individual exercises?" A few of the most haunted-looking owners admit that they are passing so far but that their dogfriend likes to lie down for a rest during the long sit, or likes to inspect the rest of the line for bitches in season during the long down. From there the conversation rapidly deteriorates into a series of obedience horror stories, a confessional of classes almost passed, of dogs that have earned two legs in sixteen trials, of high hopes and improbable failures. The Open A group is the only place that a trainer will admit that it took twenty trials for his dog to earn a degree. Most dogs do not take nearly so long but a few do, and so long as the owner does not give up, the dog will eventually pass and finish the degree. The Open A group teaches the value of perseverance. The conversation is all immediate. It concerns the present class and dogs, the degrees in progress, and the immediate problems.

Open B owners seldom mention what is happening in their class during the group. They discuss training methods—who is trying a new approach and how it is working. They discuss

*See Appendix for an explanation of terminology used in this book.

and evaluate recent obedience articles. They analyze problem dogs and offer possible alternate techniques for their handler's use. The handlers in Open B are a varied group during the off (non-dog-show) lives. There are grandmothers and junior handlers, schoolteachers and doctors, housewives and policemen. They generally have more than one, but fewer than five, dogs. One or two are current competition dogs, one is usually a retired veteran, and generally the next generation is in training. The people in Open B are the repeaters, the steady competitors who are not working just on a degree; most of their dogs have not only C.D.X.s but also U.D.s. They are working on the annual top-dog standings, and their dedication is incredible. When one is working for top dog in a working or sporting breed, every score helps. Many of the regulars attend more than ninety percent of the shows in their area. The group spends virtually every weekend together. The dogs and handlers working on obedience titles come and go just as most show dogs vanish after completing their championships. The Open B—Utility B dogs are the equivalent of the campaigned champions. They are at every show, accumulating rating points and trying for High in Trial, as breed dogs pursue Best in Show.

Learning From the Dog

Most training books urge the trainer to be patient. For a lesson in patience, observe the dog's example. Dogs are incredibly patient with our whims. They submit to our rather fumbling first experiments in dog training. While we think that we are teaching them, they will teach us if we only have the eye to watch them and enough humility to learn from them. The more sentimental readers may not approve of the analogy, but the dog is like a computer terminal. When we have a clever theory on training, we run it by the dog for testing and the dog either accepts or rejects it. Either the theory computes or it does not. If it does, then it is mentally filed along with other successful methods. If it fails, then it joins the growing collection of abandoned theories.

How does one come up with new theories to submit to the dog test? Trainers swap theories while waiting at ringside, or during the Open B exercises. They study training books and books on dog psychology and pack behavior. The chapters on puppy mental development in Clarence Pfaffenberger's *The New Knowledge of Dog Behavior* should be essential reading for anyone who is interested either in training dogs or in raising puppies with the best possible temperaments. In general the animal behavior books are more interesting than the training books. The behavior analysis books are also useful for the next step, which is to create new theories by studying your own dog. He can teach you more than you can teach him, starting with patience and going on to attention.

Attention

Most dogs and owners meander through life in a comfortable, slightly daydreaming state, taking each other for granted. Even so, the dog is incredibly aware of his owner. Every move, tone of voice, and shift in facial expression is noted by the dog. How many trainers can say that they read their dogs half so well as the dogs read them? "Reading" a dog is a process of observing the dog's behavior, body language, and facial expressions and, from these, understanding what the dog is thinking. This is an area where practice makes one increasingly good, but never quite perfect. Dogs have a wide and individual repertoire of body language. They also have perfectly readable facial expressions. If your dog's face is invisible beneath a mop of hair you become an expert on body language.

Do you doubt that dogs have truly expressive faces? Sunny could make a believer out of anyone. We were practicing the stand for examination for Utility. Sunny is a fidgeter and this was a tough exercise for her. She was next to last in line and managed to hold still until the class trainer examined her and started to turn away. On the side farthest from him, she quickly moved a back foot foreward two inches, but she was too soon and he saw her. He came back. He moved the foot to its original position and gave her an entirely token slap on the rump to remind her not to move again, at least not while he was watching. Her feet and body completely immobilized, she slowly turned her head to face him and bestowed on him the dirtiest look I have ever seen from dog or person. She silently and eloquently told him, "Why you nasty old man— Keep your hands off my fanny. How dare you?" The trainer and I both broke out laughing at the intensity of her disgust. It would have stopped any neighborhood lecher in his tracks.

When the handler tries to concentrate his attention on the dog to read it better, he will become aware of how intensely the dog is observing him. Most handlers have numerous unconscious habits which are so routine that they are beneath notice—except that the dog does notice them. Many dogs have been failed in the ring because they correctly responded to their handlers' unconscious cues. It is then said that the dog failed. Notice the terminology. Handlers exhibit, but dogs fail. Somehow this places the blame on the dog, but the dog may not have been in the wrong. It may have answered a cue that the handler was unaware of. The only way to prevent this kind of failure is for the handler to become aware of every action he takes while in the ring or practicing. This is as difficult as it sounds. The handler has to concentrate both on the dog and on himself, to a degree that he is unaccustomed to. It takes extensive practice, and it helps to have another person point out the unconscious cues until the handler can spot them for himself.

It is important to analyze failures for their causes. Often on the way home from a trial the reason for a dog's behavior suddenly will become clear. Where originally it was puzzling, it will suddenly flash and be perfectly understandable. At least, it will be perfectly understandable from the dog's point of view. My favorite failure was on what would have been my Greyhound bitch's third Utility leg. She dropped very nicely to my hand signal in the middle of the long stand. Was the signal deliberate? Not at all, I was just trying to recapture an annoying loose strand of hair on a windy day, but, from the dog's point of view, it was a perfectly valid hand signal. She was right.

Often sheer relief will unsettle a handler. If a dog almost fails an exercise but manages to struggle through and pass it, the chances are quite high that the next exercise will be failed. Why? Because the handler is so distracted by the near miss that he then miscues the dog. For example, after successfully completing a very touch-and-go directed retrieve exercise, I praised the dog. At the same time, I unintentionally gave him the command word that sent him out of the ring and he was failed for leaving the ring. Was it embarrassing? Well yes, I had sent him directly into a waiting group of members from my obedience club which included the chief instructor. Ick. Did the dog come back? He came back instantly, and on the first command. If he had been moving at less than his usual speed, he might have been within the ring rope when he turned to come back and finish the class.

The better a worker the dog is, the more observant he is. The better the trainer is, the more observant he becomes of both the dog and of himself. The ultimate goal is a team, each half of which is under alert conscious control, responding to clear clues, and totally in contact with each other. Does this sound like drudgery? Actually it is delightful, and it cannot be attained through conventional adversary-style training methods. If the training is dull, the result will be a slow-working, bored dog. If the training is overly corrective, the result will be a slow-working or non-working, flighty dog. Few dogs can be forced into being excellent. All dogs can be invited into a partnership in which they play a game called

Does obedience training ruin a dog for breed showing? Properly taught, obedience will help the dog show well. This is Champion Clairidge Light Fantastic on a Utility stand stay.

training. The game is made up of friendly instruction with maximum encouragement, a minimum of understanding corrections, and a great variety of playful practice.

For People Without Time to Train

Training instructors often urge students to train eight days a week. Few people have the time available to do so. Fewer dogs have the concentration to put up with it. With this method I have trained dogs to C.D.s by the time they were seven months old and to U.D.s by the time they were twenty months old. But here is the catch: By the time those dogs were two years old, I had become bored and the dogs were retired. It is often said that overexposure makes a dog ring-sour and his performance deteriorates. What really happens is that overexposure bores the handler, and the dog reflects

the handler's mood. As long as the handler can maintain his
enthusiasm, the willing dog will perform well. In contrast, I
have taken six months to teach a dog Novice and a year
teaching it Open, training for a few minutes once or twice a
week. The dogs and I both find this latter system much more
enjoyable than the fast method. The key to it is that dogs
have excellent memories which are not wiped clean by a few
days or weeks of inactivity. A dog will remember indefinitely
anything that he enjoys. The handler just has to remember
how far they have progressed. Now what owner can say that
he does not have time to train a dog for a few minutes twice a
week? True, this leisurely schedule will not fit in with a
formal obedience class. While I am an obedience club
member and we spend a good deal of time visiting classes, we

*Ch. Clairidge Light Fantastic again, this time in the hands of one
of the countries top breed handlers. A stand stay is the same
exercise whether it is done with a handler's guidance or as a free
stand for obedience. (Photo by Rich Bergman)*

Does obedience ruin a dog for field events? Again the answer is no. It does give the owner useful control of the dog. Sunny was the first Greyhound bitch to earn a Utility Dog title.

After receiving her obedience title, Sunny took up lure coursing, where she quickly became a Field Champion. She then became the first Greyhound to be awarded the Lure Courser of Merit title. For two years she was the only Greyhound to hold that title. Obedience has interfered in no way with her field performance.

do not enroll in them because of their inflexible time schedules. Instead the dogs are trained individually, at leisure, and we then use the classes as a source of distractions to accustom the dog to working in the presence of strange dogs and unexpected events. The class is not the place to teach a dog an unfamiliar exercise. Faced with both a new routine and the distractions, the dog has too great a chance of making a wrong choice and of being corrected. The dog should have every conceivable chance of succeeding in a new exercise so that you can praise him. The owner should help him succeed and, if necessary, trick him into succeeding.

If you want to use a training class to learn teaching aids, consider taking a substitute dog to it, not the dog you are seriously interested in training. A retired member of the household could benefit from the practice. If you are involved in dog rescue work, a rescue dog can be made much more suitable for adoption after two months of letting you practice on him in the Novice class. In my teenage days the shelter was on my way home from school. My understanding parents tolerated a steady flow of rescued Collies and German Shepherds, with each dog trained through Novice before being placed in a home. The training solved the problem of dogs that shuttle through homes due to lack of manners on the dog's part and lack of control on the new owner's part. The trained dogs all stayed where they were placed.

Whether you decide to train on your own or start with a class, it should not be a burden. Work out a routine that fits in with your normal lifestyle. There are owners who have taught heeling in their front rooms. I teach most of scent discrimination in the den. Be inventive.

Instructors and Training Classes

The handler who is new to dog training may choose to look for a good training class. Classes are often run either by nonprofit training clubs or by individuals. In either case what the handler should look for is quality instruction and a humane approach to training. Classes are usually run continuously. As soon as one class graduates, another is enrolled. Go and watch the class in progress before you enroll for a later series. Do the class dogs look happy? Are they willing workers? Do the owners look happy? Good. On the other hand, are people shouting at and abusing dogs? If they are, find another class. If you intend to participate in A.K.C. competition try to find an instructor who does compete. Many instructors direct their efforts toward helping owners combat the large unruly dog population and are not really familiar with obedience competition. Only a small minority of the dogs enrolled in training classes ever sees the inside of an A.K.C. obedience trial ring.

The training sessions of most classes last for an hour or two, long enough to bore most dogs thoroughly. I used to take a pair of dogs and trade off during the session, with the instructor's permission.

Graduation

Many dogs enrolled in training classes fail their graduation test, which makes the handlers feel disappointed. They should not be. In a six- to ten-week training class there is only time to teach the basic exercises. The dog comprehends the meaning of the exercises but he has not had time to develop the habit of responding correctly every time. In addition, most beginning handlers are very tense at graduation time. With that combination it is a wonder that anyone passes.

GENERAL TRAINING HINTS
Pace and Speed

Next to talking to a heeling dog the best thing a handler can do to help the dog is to walk quickly. The dog should have to move out of a walk and heel at an easy trot in order to keep up with the handler. A bored dog shows passive resistance by slowing down. If the handler slows his pace to match the dog's, the dog will slow down still further, until finally both of them are creeping along. If, instead of slowing down, the handler moves faster, he makes heeling more interesting for the dog. Keeping up becomes a challenge that keeps the dog awake during the heeling.

Friends

If the dog and trainer are friends to begin with, there is no need to sacrifice that friendship just because the trainer thinks that the dog is working poorly on a given day. Many trainers have unrealistically high expectations, not for the final degree of perfection, but for the time it will take to reach that point. As long as the dog is working happily and making progress, even if it seems to be leisurely progress, the trainer should be pleased instead of impatient. Dogs do have off days. They also go through cycles where they regress and then improve again on a given exercise completely independent of the trainer's efforts. In fact, the best thing the trainer can do in such a situation is relax and take a short vacation.

Training Time

In a thirty-minute training session the dog has plenty of slack time to think up new and different ways to brighten up the exercises. The dog creates his own versions of the exercises, and most of his private versions will not agree with the A.K.C. formula for success. This leads to frustrated owners and playful dogs. The owners whimper, "I don't understand why he does that to me in the ring. I know that he knows the exercises." He does that to you in the ring because he has been bored during his training. It did not hold his interest. He would rather show you a new and different variation than run through the same old exercises once more. At least if he throws in a new twist his handler will react in an entertaining way.

When the trainer is teaching a new exercise in playtraining, the maximum schedule for the training sessions would be three times a week for about fifteen minutes each. The dog should have a basic understanding of the exercise in no more than three weeks. Then the training time for that exercise drops to a couple of minutes' practice twice a week.

The Handler's Progress

With each dog a handler trains, his training skills increase. His ability to read the dog improves. He becomes able to give increased amounts of positive reinforcement to the dog. His physical coordination improves. (Some training procedures are just plain awkward when they are first attempted.) The trainer becomes more lively and animated with each dog. His timing improves greatly, and good timing is one of the greatest assets a trainer can have. Making the appropriate response at the proper moment is the goal, and the proper moment is just as important as the appropriate response.

The Run-Through

Never routinely run through all the class exercises every time you train. A run-through is precisely that—once through to let the dog get used to performing the different exercises in sequence. It is not the place to train a dog on the basic exercises. Extended training on any exercise before going on to the next defeats the purpose of the run-through, which is to establish smooth transitions from one exercise to the next. If the dog gets stuck on a particular exercise, repeat it once if you can think of a way to help the dog perform correctly. If not, go on by and finish the rest of the run-through. The next time you train on individual exercises, try the one that the dog had trouble with. If he still cannot manage it but once was able to do it, stop. *Do not keep repeating a failure*. All that is accomplished by repeating a failure is to teach the dog to fail. It decreases his self-confidence and gives him increased cause to remember the wrong way of doing the exercise. You can program failure into a dog as easily as success.

The Magic Trick

Often the best training is no training. When a dog gets stuck in a learning block, it is really impressive to see what a week off can do to clear his mind. In severe cases a month or even several months may help. That does not mean you stop training. It is not as if he has to learn one particular exercise before he can go on to the next stage in his training. There are dozens of exercises. Teach him several new ones. Then one day reintroduce the one he had the block about. Just casually give him the direction as if you expected him to do it successfully. More than half the time he will then do it just as if he had never had any problem with it. The dogs seem to think things over on their days off and solve their own problems. Either that or, after the first failure, they become so apprehensive about possibly failing again that they can no longer figure out the right way to perform and keep failing until you take the pressure off of them. The rest gives them a breather in which they regain their self-confidence.

The Sound Dog

In dog-show terms a sound dog is one that is built so that he trots correctly. In obedience a sound dog has nothing to do with leg structure. It is a dog that will perform an exercise reliably even when exposed to distractions such as unfamiliar surroundings or strange dogs. A dog at class graduation time may know the exercises, but he will not be sound. Another four to eight weeks of practice is needed to produce a sound working dog, especially in the Open and Utility classes. This practice is done in the presence of distractions. Obedience clubs in large urban areas hold frequent practice matches which provide all the distractions that a trainer could ask for. Trainers in more remote areas have to invent their own distractions. There is a local trainer who likes to have me run my greyhounds in the park while he is training his Bouvier des Flandres. Two greyhounds playing tag are an excellent distraction.

The Wrong Correction

There is a tendency to try to make a correction so unforgettable that the dog will never make the same mistake again. If a correction is so strong that the dog never forgets it, there is a good chance that he also will not forget the exercise that led up to the correction, and he will try to avoid that exercise. The dog is not wrong when you correct him. Wrongness is only your value judgment. The dog is just not doing what you want him to, and the correction is one way of bringing about the response you desire. Correction is guidance. *It should not be punishment.* The quickest way to make a dog think that even a mild correction is punishment is to add a verbal reproof to it. The collar correction may not tell the dog much about the handler's feelings, but if the handler says "Rotten puppy!" along with the correction, the dog knows that it is being punished. Many well-intentioned handlers verbally abuse their dogs in the mistaken belief that this is kinder than a physical correction. Steady verbal abuse is the surest way of destroying a dog's self-confidence.

The Correct Correction

The proper correction is given with or immediately followed by enthusiastic praise. After all, if the correction worked, the dog is doing the right thing and deserves praise for his current correct behavior. The leash correction itself is not a strong yank on the leash. It is a very quick, moderately firm tug that tightens the training collar suddenly and immediately releases it. This creates a quick pop on the neck. The idea is to startle the dog. You are trying to surprise the dog, not cause him pain. If he gets corrected all the time, it is not going to surprise him. If he is used to being talked through the exercises and working on a loose leash, then the quick, light pop on the neck is all the correction he will need. It wakes him up, gets his attention, and he can then bask in the accompanying praise.

The Best Correction

The best correction is no correction at all. This means guiding or even tricking the dog into being right, so that he can be praised and reinforced for his correct behavior.

The Second Chance Correction

Let us talk for a moment about correction, force, and punishment. Once a trainer is sufficiently practiced to praise the dog for a good performance, then the alternative is to punish a poor performance, right? Wrong! The alternative is to provide guidance, to use the least possible force, and to give the dog a second chance to perform correctly. When an exercise is first taught, the dog will not perform the same way each time he is cued. While still in the learning process the dog is searching out the possible actions available to him. In the go away he may go out ten feet, make a sudden turn, and head off in an unexpected direction. In the drop on recall he will occasionally miss the drop cue and come straight in. He may try heeling on the handler's right side. He may step on the broad jump. The dog is not committing errors; he is exploring the alternate solutions to each exercise, and this exploration is part of the learning process. Discipline at this point may compel him to do the exercise, but it will also confuse and discourage him about the educational process. Instead of being punished after one of these experiments, the dog should be taken back to the exercise's starting point with a wistful, "Silly, if you are going to do it that way, then you are going to have to try it again." And he gets a second chance, having been neither praised nor punished for the erratic first attempt. My dogs quickly learned to recognize that an instant replay of an exercise without praise means the first performance was not a success. Praise is what they are seeking, and if they do not get it they try another method on the second attempt. When they get it right, they are rewarded with the expected praise *and a change in activities*. This can be either the end of the training session, or a chance to run and play, or just a change to a different exercise.

My ideal of an obedience dog is one that, when presented with a new training situation, starts a search through a variety of possible responses to it until he receives praise for one of them. Then he concentrates on the variation that has brought him the praise. The more confidence the dog has in himself and his trainer, the more alternatives he will try before giving up, and therefore the greater is his chance of finding the desired response. The trainer helps by guiding the dog in finding the correct response, by encouraging him to keep trying, and by praising him when the goal is reached. Reinforcement is a much more useful training tool than force. The use of force makes a dog afraid to be wrong instead of desirous of being right and receiving praise. The only way for the dog never to be wrong is for him to do nothing and show no initiative, and the dogs that are smart enough to recognize this become the passive-resistance dogs, the slow and reluctant workers.

The only force that is particularly beneficial in training is the one defined in George Lucas's *Star Wars*, where "The Force is an energy field created by all living things; it surrounds us and binds this galaxy together." In this sense it is the shared companionship, intelligence, humor, and affection between living creatures, between dog and trainer. In this sense, "May the Force be with you"—and your dog.

The Shy Dog

An apprehensive or frightened or worried dog is too busy being worried to be able to think his way through an obedience exercise. This makes the shy dog one of the most challenging dogs to train. A shy dog's attention is largely directed inward at his own imaginary fears. This leaves very little of his learning ability free to respond to his trainer. When one is training a shy dog, punishment is even more useless than usual. At a certain rather low level of panic the dog's mind freezes and it is impossible to get any information into it. The shy dog who falls on his back and offers his throat, saying, "Go ahead and kill me. I know that I deserve it," has just totally defeated his trainer. At that moment he can be taught nothing. The trainer, having been effectively defeated by a dog, has a natural inclination towards anger. After all, the dog has won that round. In order to be able to help the dog, the trainer needs, at this point, to be able to say *cheerfully*, "Hey, silly, get up. Come on. Let's go heel—or go for a romp," or do anything different from what they were doing when the dog was frightened. With practice the handler can learn to tell when the dog is being pressed too hard and back off before the training becomes so serious and overwhelming to the dog that he panics.

Besides the dog that is shy in training there is the problem of the dog that is shy of people. There is a strange and almost unvarying human reaction to a shy dog. When the dog stands back from a stranger, the person insists on proving his friendliness by advancing on the dog. The problem here is that when one dog advances slowly towards another it is an act of aggression, and the shy dog sees the advancing stranger as an aggressor. What may have been only caution turns into genuine fright. If the dog is prevented from fleeing, if he is tied or crated, he can easily be put into a state of hysteria. This phenomenon accounts for a fair amount of fear biting. It could be avoided if only people could resist the urge to invade the shy dog's personal defense perimeter. Every dog has a fight-flight boundary. Faced with a threat that is outside the boundary the dog will watch it carefully, give an alarm bark, and try to frighten it off. When the threatening form crosses the fight-flight boundary, the dog has to take action either to flee or defend itself. If you really want to prove that you are a friend to a shy dog, back off, sit down, and talk quietly. Decreasing your apparent size reduces the threat you present. If there is a braver dog handy, pet it and ignore the shy dog. Especially avoid eye contact. An outgoing dog will seek eye contact. A shy dog considers it a threat, which (among dogs) it is. How long it will take for the dog to come to you depends on just how shy he is. If you do not have enough time to outwait the dog, give up gracefully and leave him unfrightened. If you have a shy dog and see well-intentioned strangers advancing purposefully, insist that they stand back and let the dog come to them. Then be prepared to have them ignore your first request and try to advance on the dog anyway.

Responsibility to the Dog

One of the greatest attractions of obedience training is that it tends to stabilize a person's dog population. Once a dog and owner have worked together up to even the companion dog level, that dog has earned pet status. As used here, pet status is not a derogatory term. A well-known dog breeder once earnestly told me that none of her dogs was a pet. She was not talking about pet quality. She actually meant that none of them was her pet. What a pity. The lady is denying herself one of the most agile-minded and responsive and certainly one of the warmest dogfriends possible. For what reason? To be a businesslike breeder. To refuse to become so attached to a dog that it could not be sold or moved out to make room for a promising newcomer.

Many members of the dog fancy are caught in the promising-puppy trap. In search of a winner they buy a puppy. But puppies are a gamble, not an investment. They are a hope for the future. What the buyer is purchasing is a dream and a possibility. The only sure thing about any puppy is that it will grow into a dog with varying degrees of faults. Since there are very few truly outstanding dogs, a large number of puppies grow up less than perfect. The dog fancier caught in the puppy trap becomes disenchanted with the grown dog sometime around its second birthday and acquires a new promising puppy to dream on. The grown dog has become surplus and is disposed of. The owner has never had a personal relationship with the dog. The dog was a prop for the owner's fantasies. Obedience training assists the owner in establishing an understanding of and working relationship with the dog. Obedience makes the dog a real living friend to the owner instead of a fantasy object. It also makes the dog easier to live with. Dogs with manners and a reasonable command of our language are comfortable companions.

One of the measures of a dog's worth is the amount of time that the owner has invested in him. The more training time that is put into a dog, the more attached the owner becomes to that dog. The effort that an owner puts into the training creates a debt and bond between him and the dog that makes it hard to separate the two casually. Breed champions are bought and sold, often rather cheaply. If you would like to see an interesting human reaction and are prepared to face some incredulous laughter, offer to buy someone's Utility dog.

Even small amounts of training will greatly reduce the turnover in the dog population. By the time it becomes apparent that a growing puppy will never be the number-one dog of its breed, the perceptive owner may realize that he is nonetheless still a first-class dog, friend, and companion, and that is all that the dog ever wanted to be. So here is a kind word for dogs as pets and companions to man. No dog is born trained. He is what the handler makes of him, either adversely through neglect or beneficially through work, care, and training. No dog is perfect in the show sense, but every dog can be perfect in the eyes of a loving owner. The dogs deserve better from us than to be shunted off to a series of temporary homes as two-year-olds. If having a winner is more important than having a dog, the fancier should buy an adult dog who is a winner. It will not be any more expensive than buying and raising three puppies, and it is the only sure way to obtain a winner.

This is not to say that every dog a person acquires should die with that person. It is possible for a dog to be temperamentally or emotionally mismatched to its home, and such a dog could be better off in a different environment. But transfers of this nature are insignificant when compared with the number of dogs cast off for lack of discipline or for being show rejects.

Solitary

The ultimate method of providing motivation for the grown dog is isolation in varying degrees. We can smother a dog with our constant presence until he takes us for granted and is not particularly interested in us. The easiest way to regain the dog's attention is by separating the dog from us. Absence in this case does indeed make the heart grow fonder. It also makes the dog more alert and responsive. For this technique the dog does not need to be sent off to a kennel. What is needed to reactivate the dog is moderate separation and a little benign neglect. The far end of my yard has a fenced section where in-season bitches are kept company by fifteen-year-old Traveler. Because the gate is fifty feet from the back door, and I am fairly lazy, the distance reduces my contact with whichever dogs are in residence. These dogs are cared for several times and run once a day, but they do not have their usual opportunities to crowd into the kitchen dog corner and sit on my foot while I cook dinner or to try to sneak into the bedroom. Consequently they consider residence in the far yard to be exile.

When overexposure dulls a dog's enthusiasm, he goes to live with Traveler, who is not a great deal of fun for an active adult dog to play with. Within two days to a week the dog is more than happy to play people (obedience) games again. In addition to being nonviolent, this method is much more successful than trying to punish a dog into working when his will to perform diminishes.

Brainwashing the Hard Case

Isolation has its uses not only in keeping a fine edge on a competition dog but also in the salvaging of dogs with severe motivation problems. For the dog whose will to please has been destroyed through mishandling, isolation may be the only approach that he will respond to. Such dogs are bored, hostile, or indifferent. They will not respond to conventional motivations because they have been taught that praise is a hollow mockery, that training is a setup to trap them into making mistakes, which are followed by punishment, and that it is not safe to concentrate on food rewards. Worry kills the appetite, anyway. These disillusioned dogs often become destructive and impossible to live with. For such dogs we are interested not in competition but in simply reforming them into companions. The word reforming is intended literally. It is necessary to *re-form* their outlook on life, to make basic changes in deeply ingrained attitudes. This is much more difficult than superficial training, and isolation is the strongest motivation technique that can be used. Isolation makes the dog dependent on the trainer not only for physical care but also for all the social contact that the dog receives, and dogs are very social animals. When a dog is sitting idle in a run for twenty-four hours a day and is taken out for training for fifteen minutes every other day, his attention focuses on that brief break in his boredom.

Lots of early contact with people and exposure to a variety of new scenery teaches a puppy to take unusual situations calmly. In this case the puppy has found herself modeling flight luggage.

This method works best on dogs that were properly socialized as puppies, so that they desire human contact but have acquired behavior problems through later mishandling. While controlled isolation will also benefit the poorly socialized dog or a dog with kennel dog syndrome, the results are not as dramatic as with a well-socialized dog. It is not surprising that this method should work on dogs. The North Koreans used it with considerable success on prisoners of war.

Training Age

There are many fine myths to the effect that a dog should not be trained until he is one year old. These myths were started because an older dog has a longer attention span and greater tolerance for corrections, which means the trainer has to work less carefully than he does with a puppy. When I train dogs for friends, I prefer dogs at least eight months old. However, a dog is actually capable of learning anytime after the age of three weeks, and my own dogs are conditioned from that age. This is not formal training. At first it is simple imprinting of the human presence on the dog. It is easy to tuck a well-fed puppy in the crook of an arm while reading or watching television. When the puppy is six weeks of age, this turns into puppy play, encouraging him to chase and come to me for mock wrestling matches and hair-biting games. When the puppy's vaccinations are complete it is time to take him out to meet the public, taking along a calm older dog to set a good example. When they are in the cute puppy stage, there is no shortage of people to help socialize the dogs. A pair of puppies at the beach or down at the shopping mall soon attract their own circle of volunteer petters who think that I am doing them a favor by letting them touch the puppies. It is, incidentally, considerably easier to raise a pair of puppies than just one. They provide companionship, exercise, and entertainment for each other. While pairs of the same sex will often scuffle as adults, a brother-sister pair can grow up into the kind of devoted fellowship that my greyhounds, Sunny and Tiger, show each other. By the time the puppies are three months old, we start gradual and low-key Novice

Puppy love is a lick on the nose. This is the same greeting the puppy would use with an adult dog. After all, a puppy spends much of its early life being licked by its mother, and one lick deserves another.

training with lots of play. The conditioning from three weeks to three months is used to develop the dog's personality, orient it toward people, and instill in it confidence and the desire to please. A stable temperament and the desire to please are the most important assets to later training.

Pack Behavior

Anyone with more than two dogs has a pack. Even the person with fewer than three dogs will see elements of pack behavior in the dogs' relationships with each other and with their owner. Pack behavior is often anthropomorphized and misinterpreted. Horrors, the puppy grew up to fight with his father and brothers! Or the pack gangs up to reject a misfit member. As much as this bothers us, with our human code of behavior, dogs have been running with packs considerably longer than they have been running with people. In fact most dog-master relationships are based on the dog's ability to substitute a person for the pack leader. We will not investigate what the person is substituting the dog for. From the dog's point of view he is still operating within the rules of pack behavior. Since that is the case, it is to our advantage to understand how a pack functions.

The pack's major interests are food, sex, play, and dominance. For the domesticated dog, food is provided and sex is hopefully controlled by the owner. This leaves the domestic pack free to concentrate on its social relationships. An understanding of the functions of both play and dominance is essential to obedience training. Play is generally either mock-fighting or mock-hunting. The practice hunt can be one of the most successful forms of incentive for obedience. Whether the owner knows it or not, he has a place in the dominance order of his pack, so it is a good idea to learn about dominance. Otherwise, you are engaged in a game without knowing the rules.

Play

Novice obedience can be taught with simple praise as reward. For the voluntary exercises beyond Novice, the dog needs a motivation that can be given at a distance from the handler. The strongest possible incentive for hunting dogs is pursuit. The chase has been bred into them literally right down to their toes. Why shouldn't we use that five thousand years of bred-in instinct to motivate them for the comparatively new sport of obedience? This means getting the dog to play, and, in some cases, actually teaching him to play. The objective here is to produce what Whippet owners would call a good rag dog, a dog that will fanatically pursue an

For the shy dog the handler may need to lie down before the dog can get up enough courage to play. To a dog, height is power, and having the handler come down to the dog's level will reassure the dog.

artificial quarry. All that is needed is some open space and a few rabbit skins (direct from Korea for $1 each at the local import store, for city dwellers like me). Some dogs will grab and "kill" a pelt the first time they see it, but many will not. Then the owner gets to play with the "bunny," to toss it in the air, catch it, shake it, and romp with the dog. The lure is thrown short distances ahead of the dog. The first time the owner may have to race the dog to the lure, beat him to it, and pick it up. Dogs like to play "keep away." Eventually the dog will win the race, or he may take the lure out of the owner's hands and run with it. Once a pack has one good rag dog his enthusiasm is contagious. The others learn from his example.

Every dog can be taught to play. Some may catch on instantly, but some may take months. I had almost given up on the white bitch in this photo. Her low pack status so inhibited her that she was unable to play with me although she could play with some of the lower ranked dogs. When playing the rag games, the other dogs would never let her have the bunny. As a last resort I took her out alone and simply lay down in the park. This often works with insecure dogs. To dogs, height is status. The strongest dog stands tallest. This dog had never seen me shorter than she was. Having me flat on the ground removed her inhibitions, and she went wild. She started running and playing with an intensity that I've seen in few other dogs. It is a rather odd game. Basically the handler just lies down. The elbows are up to keep the dog clear of the handler's face. (The dog is moving at very high speed, and could easily misjudge a foot placement.) The dog does all the playing while the handler encourages it with peculiar little whines and whimpers. Why do it? Well, it is fun. It shows an unknown side of the dog's personality. Most importantly, since we started the game she has gained enough confidence to hang onto her end of the bunny when the other dogs try to take it, and to start to behave like a proper rag dog.

After learning to play with her handler, Kitty Hawk became confident enough to play with her dominant litter sister.

Anything Friendly That Works Is Worth Trying

Anything that does not work for a particular dog—and that includes any suggestions I may make here—should be rejected, and the trainer should keep searching for a method that works for his own dog.

Dominance

A pack with multiples of each sex will have a separate dominance ranking for dogs and bitches. The top dog and top bitch generally get along quite well with each other. The top dog defends his position against challenges from what is usually his second in command. Dogs from the bottom strata of the pack do not challenge the leader. They work their way up through the levels of the pack until only the leader is left above them. Then they try for the leadership. This does not usually mean a dog fight. Dogs have an intricate series of competitions that establish ranking among themselves.

For instance, in a pack that started with two puppies and a retired coursing dog, the scenario went like this: As a youngster, the low ranking dog was the male puppy, Tiger. His sister could outrun him, and the grown dog could outrun both of them. With adolescence, Tiger moved up one notch when he became both larger than his sister and able to show a slight speed edge on straightaway power runs. At ten months of age, he started a game that I totally misunderstood. He took to making sudden runs at the coursing dog. The objective was to hit the older dog behind the shoulder and roll him over. I was indignant. Where was Tiger's respect for age? My protests were ineffective, and by the end of the month the older dog had become a master at giving Tiger a broadside target and then pivoting at the last moment to let him charge on by. By that time the game was tapering off, and I finally realized what had been happening. The game ended because it had served its purpose. For the first time Tiger was top dog in the pack, having taken the

This is a pushing contest to determine which dog is dominant over the other. The trainer can use the same body language to dominate a dog without using force.

position without a growl or snap. He took it with tests of strength and speed. When he was clearly faster and stronger, the old dog yielded the leadership.

If a dog's activity is so restricted that he cannot use speed and strength as a means for determining rankings, he is likely to resort to fighting. Very little space is needed for a fight.

Dogs check constantly to see if the pack rankings have changed. The photo is of a pair of two-year-old litter sister bitches who are checking their rank. The raised heads, ears, hackles, and tails signal aggression as they stand as tall as they can and push against each other's necks in a strength test. The parti-color is the stronger and heavier of the two and initiated the challenge, but the fawn bitch is dominant. In the picture the parti-color has started to drop her head and tail in submission and is giving ground. This illustrates the reason why, if you stand tall and stare at a dog, it will usually drop its head or turn its head to the side to break eye contact and acknowledge your dominance. It is assumed that the dog does acknowledge the person's dominance and that the owner is the pack leader. That is not always the case.

The Trainer As Pack Leader

I have known several instances in which people were subordinate pack members to large male dogs. One of these dogs was a sighthound and one a working dog. Both, curiously, were from breeds developed to prey on wolves. In both situations the dog was physically stronger than the human owner. The attraction that very large dogs hold for moderate-sized people may sometimes not work out well. In either case, if the owner displeased the dog, the owner was disciplined, that is, the owner was first warned and then bitten. Having one subordinate human pack member already, neither dog was reluctant to bite strangers. Why would anyone keep such a dog? Each owner seemed to admire his dog's strength while not being terribly fond of its personality. In fact, each owner had gone through extraordinary difficulties to avoid being separated from his dog. It would seem that there is indeed a dog for every type of owner.

I strongly recommend that the owner of a pack of dogs any larger than Toy Poodles be the pack leader. The main difficulty with maintaining the leadership is that many owners do not recognize a challenge when it is offered. It will be made only by the highest ranking dog in the pack, generally a male just coming into his maturity. A challenge is not very obvious. The dog is not going to pounce on the owner in the middle of the night. Instead, one day the handler will make a normal correction and hear a quiet, calm, growl that says very clearly, "Hey you, knock it off. I do not acknowledge your authority." What he is actually doing is testing the owner's leadership, because the leader *has* the right to discipline any pack member without resistance on its part. If the handler backs off and tries to be reasonable about it, if he tries to deal with it on a human level, then he is going to fail, because the dog will not understand. If the handler does not react properly, the dog will be encouraged to continue to press for leadership. The correct way to respond is exactly the way a canine pack leader would (short of biting the dog in the throat). Given either a leash or a hold on the dog's collar, the handler jerks the dog flat on his side on the ground, slaps him on the shoulder, and screams at him a lot. When the dog yields, he will stop struggling and expose his throat. This is the only circumstance under which I would recommend either striking or verbally abusing a dog, and it is in a good cause. The objective is not to hurt him but to demonstrate that he ranks second on the dominance ladder. A dog will only try for leadership with its owner once or twice in its life, and once the test is over, there should be no hard feelings.

This whole subject is a touchy one. Most obedience books ignore it entirely in the hope that it will vanish. That is because of a lack of understanding. The challenge is a perfectly normal occurrence in a dog pack. The dog is simply checking to see how much status he can gain. We emotionalize it into a personal attack on us. The challenge does not mean that the dog does not love the owner. The dog does indeed love the owner and will continue to love him whether the dog wins and the owner becomes a subordinate pack member or whether the owner wins and the dog settles into number two rank. The event has nothing to do with affection or with cruelty. It is a very simple and direct power play. If the owner truly loves the dog he will not let the dog win.

All dogs come equipped with an impressive array of teeth. We rely on the dog's sound disposition to keep us safe from them, because the well-adjusted dog is inhibited from biting us. All dogs are not well adjusted.

Actually the dog is much better off testing leadership with his owner than he would be with another dog. When these tests occur between two dogs, they can easily result in thirty stitches for each participant, generally in the neck and shoulder area. For this reason, if the highest ranked dog should ever be badly injured, he should be separated from the pack lest one of the members decide to displace the leader while he is incapacitated. If all this sounds dreadful, it is because it is being interpreted by human standards. It is perfectly normal for the dogs, and it is not fair to judge them by our behavior standards.

A Word of Caution

Maintaining pack leadership in the face of a challenge by a dog who is just testing its strength and yours is something that most people can cope with readily once they understand what is happening. *Taking* leadership away from a large dog that has been allowed to dominate people and bite them with impunity is a high-risk venture. This kind of dog is not inhibited when it comes to biting people and it will defend its leadership privileges energetically. While it is possible to demote such a dog from pack leader to second in command, it usually takes two people and special techniques to do it safely. If you are faced with this problem get *expert* assistance. Do not challenge a dominant dog alone, particularly if the dog is larger than you are. Even medium-sized dogs have an impressive array of teeth and are physically capable of inflicting a lot of damage on anything as soft-skinned as a human being. The reason that most dogs live their entire lives without using their teeth on a person is that the well-adjusted dog is inhibited against using his teeth against members of his own pack. The dogs' own rules of behavior and social structure keep us safe from the full use of his teeth.

The difficulty here is that most people are so used to having dogs show restraint that they assume that all dogs are harmless. Give a dog the end of a beef shin bone and watch him literally grind the bone into bonemeal. Then appreciate just how much restraint the normal dog shows in not using his teeth on us.

Depriving a large dog of its established dominance without getting someone bitten requires a very knowledgeable dog handler. Do not attempt it alone. Get competent help.

Dogs use their teeth to communicate a wide range of ideas. Puppies lick and nibble at the muzzles of adult dogs both to beg food from them (in the wild, the adult dog would regurgitate food for the puppy) and to inhibit totally the adult dog's biting reflexes. Puppies generally treat people as they would adult dogs.

Dogs of all ages will bite each other gently on the throat when they are playing.

One of my friends has a pair of dogs with individual biting greetings. Her Golden Retriever will gently retrieve me into the house by proudly holding my elbow in his mouth. I find that preferable to her Belgian shepherd, whose idea of a greeting is a brisk nip on the rump, rather as if the dog were herding sheep. Although the forms of the greeting differ, what both dogs are saying is, "Hi there, glad to see you."

An undoggy visitor once flinched back from Sunny in horror, saying, "She tried to bite me." I then had a chance to explain that when an excited dog wants to play it may well do what Sunny had done: drop down on its elbows in a bow, while wagging its tail, and as in Sunny's case, turn its head *away* from the person and snap its teeth together on empty air. The lady had heard the teeth close and thought "Dog bite." But all that Sunny's tooth-clacking meant is an excited, happy dog, or "Let's play."

It is time to admit that the snarling dog in the photo on page 48 is not an attack-trained greyhound. She is a bitch in season that is warning a male dog to keep his paws off her. Male readers may find her reminiscent of some of their high-school dates. She and the male dog are normally the best of friends, but for the central week of her season she spent so much time baring her teeth that her face muscles got stiff. First she would show her teeth. If he respected that, all would be well. If not, she would snarl. The next step past the snarl would be a snap in his direction that would not touch him. Her last resort would be a dramatic snarl and lunge that would end in a bite just strong enough to pinch him. He spent a discouraged week testing her defenses. By the end of the week all she had to do was lift her lip for him to ignore her. By the next week they were friends again. We call her the Vestal Virgin. While she could easily have attacked him at any point, because a sane male dog will not retaliate against a bitch, she used only the minimum force needed to discourage him. On the few occasions when he pushed her to actually nipping him, the result was a very inhibited bite, not a full-strength one.

An uninhibited bite can open up forty stitches worth of damage in seconds. It is fortunate that most dog bites are inhibited. At one dog show I found it particularly fortunate. A fellow exhibitor had a very large dog that was known for having munched a few people. In this case the dog was the pack leader and it was from a breed developed for fighting wolves. High temperatures make even good-natured dogs irritable, and this dog was not noted for his good nature. I came back to my shade to find him monopolizing my dogs' shade and water. Without thinking, I approached him from the rear, told him to move over, and bumped him in the hip. For all his size he had deceptive speed. I know how surprised wolves must have been when they first encountered members of his breed. He spun around and bit me with nice pinching, inhibited bites, twice in the body and once on the arm before I could lift a hand or his owner could pull him off. The dog knew me and had recognized my voice when I told him to move over. That is why the bites were inhibited. He was just demonstrating that he was not to be pushed around. I was impressed by his speed but not by his manners. Like most unmannerly dogs he paid a price for it. He spent a lot of time alone, since he tended to wear out his welcome with each new acquaintance. When approaching a dog of dubious temperament, let him see you. Do not surprise him from the rear.

If a dog's temperament is really poor, do not be too surprised if he bites you even if you do approach him from the front. The only occasion on which I have been bitten by a dog that was trying to do more than communicate with me, to make his point as it were, was very educational. It taught me three things. That temperament is the responsibility of the breeders who produce the dog, that there is only one really practical solution for dogs with very poor temperaments, and not to take my eyes off an untrustworthy dog.

In this case a friend who was a Great Dane breeder said that a lady had requested one of her adult dogs as a pet. She was willing to let the dog go but did not know whether his temperament was good enough for him to be safe outside the kennel. She asked me to help her test the dog to see how he would react to strangers. I readily agreed. I knew the lady's dogs and had found them to have delightful temperaments. They had the regal look of lions and the sweet dispositions of pussycats. I did not understand until later why she was concerned about the dog in question. He turned out not to be a dog of her breeding. She had purchased the dog and his brother from another breeder. I would have been more careful knowing that, because the brother was crazy. He was both aggressive and fearful, and the fact that he had seen me visiting for most of a year had done nothing to calm either his aggressiveness or his fear.

The breeder and I walked up to the four-foot paddock fence. The dog we were to test came right up to us, looking rather distrustfully at me. She petted his head and he settled down but he never looked at her. He only had eyes for me. I offered him a hand along with some dog talk. He accepted both and let me stroke his head. It was going well. A greyhound ran up to the adjoining fence and I glanced at her. The moment eye contact was broken, the Dane froze on my arm. Dogs that bite and hang on were a new experience. It was a little like having a great white shark hanging onto my arm. The teeth had very little cutting action but the pressure was tremendous. The lady was sensitive about having her dogs disciplined, and I was weighing the options of possibly losing her friendship by striking the dog on the muzzle below the eyes to make him let go, or waiting to see if she could make him release me. At her third outraged yelp he let go. In the next week, the arm turned some interesting shades of green and purple but the damage was minor, just scrapes and bruises.

The real loser was the dog. Having just failed the first part of his temperament test he was kept at the kennel, where he quickly developed a hatred for one of the female kennel helpers who was about my size and had similar long hair. Apparently he had decided that longhaired ladies were fair game, after getting in his first bite. He was put down. Who was to blame for it? His breeder was. The difference in temperaments between the rest of the kennel's dogs and these two dogs from a different breeder was striking.

How To Be a Good Pack Leader

Being a pack leader means more than dominating the other pack members. Pack leadership is a civil service job. The leader exists not for his own sense of power, but for the benefit of the pack. He sees that the pack survives, that it stays safe and fed and sheltered from the weather. He provides protection and makes the decisions that are responsible for the health, diet, comfort, safety, and activities of the pack. When a person assumes pack leadership these are the responsibilities that go with the position.

On a brisk fall day I was exercising the pack by jogging along a shoreline path with the four trotting ahead on leash like a chariot team. We passed a young family, and the father called out a frequently asked question, "Are they all yours?" But this time an answer different from the usual "Yes" occurred to me. "That is only one way of looking at it. Actually, I'm theirs." And that is the truth. The pack leader exists for the well-being of the pack, and not the other way around.

A good run will quickly dispose of anger. Never train when you are on edge.

Love and Anger

This is the time to deal with one more skeleton in the trainer's closet, another of the seldom-mentioned aspects of dog training, and that is the trainer's temper. Most dog-training books contain a contradiction. On the one hand they suggest methods that are basically physical and often hostile. On the other hand they urge the trainer never to lose his temper. There is an unfortunate peculiarity in the social nature of the human animal that makes it one of the rare pack animals not thoroughly inhibited from harming a pack member that yields in submission. In a wild wolf pack, when the loser of a dispute turns his head aside to expose his throat or grovels to expose his belly and underside, the winner is inhibited from continuing the attack. Among humans the reverse is often the case, with a display of submission driving the victor to attack harder. It brings to mind some of the grim old nature movies of baboon packs demolishing downed leopards. It is not only the dogs that have instincts. People have their own instincts, but the dog's instincts are often prettier than ours. The day will come when someone reading this book will lose his or her temper, whether it be with a dog or a child. What can be done about it? The first step is to recognize the reaction for what it is, an unpleasant but *normal* human behavior pattern. We may not like our instincts, but we are entitled to them. This is one more area where value judgments on right and wrong get in the way of understanding the phenomenon and of gaining control over it. And controlling it is much more useful than just feeling wrong and guilty after a tantrum.

With that end in view let us consider human anger as a behavior pattern that can be understood and modified just as the dog's reactions can be. In many cultures people are far more aggressive than most "wild" animals. Aside from war, people have large numbers of competitive games for the socially acceptable release of aggressions. We may even include in the list the refined dog show. A socially unacceptable method for aggression release is the abuse of dogs, children, and women. Some of the most widely read obedience books basically recommend a little animal abuse disguised as behavior modification and justified as "for the dog's own good." Well, any contact the owner has with the dog modifies its behavior to some extent. However, beginning trainers are, for the most part, nice average folk with average dogs that just need a little education. I am repelled by the situation of having amateur authorities on training urge these people to overcome their normal reluctance to hurt their dogfriends.

Violence is violence. It feeds on itself and multiplies. Ethical considerations aside, the problem with violence or anger in a training program is that it is *nonproductive*. An angry trainer is no more capable of rational thought than is a frightened dog. The best possible training progress is made when both the dog and trainer are thinking just as hard as they can. The dog has to think actively through a new series of actions before he can commit them to memory and gradually convert them to a habit.

The Miracle of Habit

It is vital to understand the commonplace but remarkable things we call habits, and also to understand those aspects of perception and learning that create new habits and change existing ones. A habit is a timesaving shortcut in the mind. A formed habit is an unconscious mental program that enables us and the dogs to perform routine tasks without conscious mental direction. Often, after a few hours of performing habitual actions and when looking back on the time spent, we may have difficulty recalling just what those activities were. People often successfully drive home in freeway traffic while operating the car almost entirely by habit and with little recollection of the trip. This lack of recollection is the reason time seems to pass much more slowly in our memories of childhood than in our recall of recent years. The very first time that an event is experienced, the mind gives it total attention. From the information it receives it creates a pattern that will be recalled each time a similar circumstance is met in the future. A child's year is filled with new experiences, and so his memory is filled with detailed recollections. However, we poorly remember events experienced through habits and so, as years go by and our stock of habits increases, we meet fewer and fewer new experiences and therefore store fewer new and intense memories. Do you remember your very first dog show or obedience trial more clearly than more recent ones? A first occurrence is remembered in great detail, while later reoccurrences are simply referenced to the first one and, with repetition, are remembered increasingly incompletely. Once a habit exists, it takes the same kind of intense, focussed thought to alter it deliberately as was required to create it originally. When we train, we form and rearrange habits in the dog, but how do the trainer's habits affect the dog? While operating from habit, we are not thinking. We are just reacting to outside cues and remembered programming. In order to improve our ability to train, we need to be free to think and learn; that is, we need not operate in a habit mode. Habits lead to routines and routines lead to boredom, which produces slow working dogs. The goal of the handler is to be thinking actively all through training. Repetition creates bored dogs. Creative and varied repetition develops trained ones. We can create variety by breaking the exercises down into a lot of different parts, by varying our enthusiasm, by mixing routines with play, by whatever ways we can invent.

Anger Eaters

The habit of reacting to certain situations with a display of anger can be altered. The owner must be under control before the dog can be. Most references just tell the owner not to get mad at the dog. Here are ways to avoid it:

Preprogramming. Memorize a single sentence that is triggered by anger. It is surprising that in the first adrenaline rush of rage, you can key into a calm and cool preprogramming thought. The sentence has to be something that you care about personally. For Trip it was, "If you punish her, you will be destroying the very thing you love most about her" (her utterly fearless confidence). For Sunny it was, "If you punish her you will find out later that she was right" (and the punishment undeserved). Both statements were simple and true and, with practice, could simply switch off anger.

Be gentle. Train by minimum force methods. Force leads to more force.

Transference. Do not train if there have been difficulties with people at work or at home earlier that day. Even though you may think you have recovered your equanimity, the training situation can reinspire suppressed hostility. Instead, take the dogs for a brisk walk or a run and let the physical activity drain off your tension.

The pack. When feeling irritable, take fewer dogs along than usual. Three well-trained Greyhounds are all I am comfortable with in a small car. They become selectively deaf to instructions and play the pack's game of "Who, me? She can't mean me," which is irritating to an owner who has been preirritated. Actually it is an amusing game in more light-hearted moments, as each dog tries to appear more innocent than the one next to it.

Time off. Take a rest from the dogs. We love them, but they require constant care, and after weeks and years, it can wear us down. Fatigue shortens tempers. The evening after a dog show I am more than ready to feed and settle them in for the night and take the evening off for any fun activity that has nothing to do with dogs. When we become slaves to our dogs, we resent it, and eventually they suffer for it. Some of us get out of the dog game in disgust, while others become overworked and grouchy.

Population control. Could you manage with fewer dogs to lighten the workload? The dog population should not be allowed to boom to the point where the dogs' care is primarily a burden instead of their company's being a pleasure.

Cool it. An auto air-conditioner does more than help dogs arrive at shows without wilting. It will also help their owner keep both his cool and his temper. Hot owners, like hot hounds, are inclined to be grumpy.

Family time. Take time to be with the dogs for simple companionship, a time when there are no performance requirements for either dog or owner. In this day of rush and hurry it helps to remember who the individual dogs are and why we love them. For me, this may be five minutes spent with them on the cushions of my kitchen dog corner; or it can be finding out that Tiger has silently disappeared from that corner. He does this by lifting his toenails up to avoid clicks on the hardwood floors and slowly drifting into the bedroom. It is easy to sit on the corner of the bed with him for a moment before taking him back to dog territory.

Alternatives to Anger. A good cry or a run in the park will relieve as much tension as having a tantrum at the dog. Any brisk physical activity will defuse anger.

Recognize transference. Learn to recognize when you are transferring emotions that have no original connection with the dog into anger at him. To cite an example and one of the turning points in my own training: After I had spent eighteen months trying to reprogram myself out of the habit of conventional adversary training methods, the turning point came unexpectedly. I was very much worried about a close friend's health. After a late night hospital visit, I returned to the car distraught to find that Trip, my nine-month-old puppy, had been nibbling on the clear plastic welting in the seams of the new seat covers. My dogs are not allowed to eat cars. Here was a perfect justification to punish her. I pounced on her, seizing her by the scruff of the neck, and for the first time in her life she gave a small surprised yelp and collapsed submissively. I had meticulously raised her as a thinking partner instead of a robot-subordinate, and the shock of seeing her in an appeasement position stopped me. In a learning moment I recognized that punishing her would be mainly a release for worries that had nothing to do with her, and that, after having spent eight months carefully building her temperament into my favorite kind of outgoing self-reliance, I was within a few minutes of destroying her faith in me. Nothing was worth that, so I extracted her from the back seat and, with a lap full of gangly nine-month-old Greyhound puppy, had a good cry against the back of her neck until she decided that she couldn't let her owner be untidy and insisted on licking the tears away. We both felt better afterward, and I was never tempted to break the trust again.

For the car-oriented readers who say, "Yes, but what happened to the seat covers?"—they never seemed very important again, but the clear welting proved irresistible even to my older, thoroughly trained dogs. The upholstery itself was not touched, but the welting was nibbled away by my Greyhounds as cleanly as if it had never been there. By the time the car was traded in, it was completely de-welted. The dogs showed no interest whatever in the new car's upholstery.

When Disobedience Is Not

Contrary to popular belief in the superiority of the human race, the owner is not always right. It is hard enough for the average person to admit that he was wrong in dealing with another person. It is still harder for someone to admit he was wrong and the dog was right, but dogs are entitled to be right occasionally. Sunny has the depressing tendency of being right whenever I find the two of us at cross-purposes.

She and I were at a dismal lure field trial to pick up the last points for her Lure Courser of Merit title. It was an undistinguished course plan set on one of the few fields where I will not normally run my dogs. But she needed only six points, so I overruled my better judgment and we were there. It is a good idea not to overrule one's better judgment. She was delighted to be there. I was disgruntled. The lure line was too worn to withstand the tension needed for greyhound speeds. After one more line failure I called Sunny back from the far end of the field. She ran back along the line while the other two dogs played with the lure. Suddenly she halted and began to spin in a tight circle. This is invariably a danger sign on a lure course. It means that the dog is caught in the line that pulls the lure. The dog spins in an attempt to escape or to reach what is hurting him. He continues to spin, wrapping the line tighter and tighter. When he whirls to face the attack from the rear, he can see nothing to fight and he is then attacked from a new position. What is attacking him is the line itself, which can burn like a hot wire, especially with two dogs pulling at the lure. I had seen a saluki with his leg sliced to the bone in the same situation. It is an infrequent occurrence, but it did not seem fair that Sunny was about to be injured after having run at thirty-five trials without a scratch.

I was running toward her and calling "Down" to immobilize her until I could get there. With each "Down" cue she gave a little dip but to my astonishment she did not go down. After six tries it occurred to me that she was not going to obey, but she appeared to be listening and to not be in a panic. So I changed the cue to "Stay." She did respond to that. It broke her spin, and she stood until I could pant up to her. A quick check of her showed no marks or cuts, and I gratefully leashed her and started back with a wry comment on my fancy obedience dog's lack of response to the down. There she was, the first Utility-titled Field Champion and the only Utility-titled Lure Courses of Merit, and she would not even lie down on cue—the most elementary Novice exercise.

We went back to the car, where she took a drink and cooled out. Then I rolled her over to tape her feet for the next run and discovered the answer to her refusal to drop. I'll never know how the line rode up that high on her, but on her belly, high in the tuck, was a network of line burns. On every down cue when she had done her curtsey to start the drop, it had brought her in contact with the line, and the pain had bounced her back up. That she would even try to drop after the third or fourth repetition was the remarkable thing. So have faith in your dog. The dogs are right more often than we give them credit for, and they are often right when they do not appear to be.

FORMING THE PARTNERSHIP BETWEEN DOG AND HANDLER
The Novice Class Exercises

Training Equipment

One of the nicest things about the Novice class is that it requires the least equipment. The essentials are:

One dog with handler.

One training (slip) collar with a six-foot lead.

One long line—between twenty to thirty feet.

One light line—three to four feet.

(Both the light line and the long line can be made out of some inexpensive sash cord available at any hardware store. To get the kinks out of it when it is new, dampen and stretch it. Tying a strong and lightweight snap to the end of each line makes things more convenient.)

The lead can be either leather or cotton webbing. Leather is easiest on the hands, although the web leads are good in wet weather when leather gets slimy and is hard to dry. Dogs will eat either type of lead. Tiger prefers leather. Sunny will not lay a tooth on leather, but she has a taste for cotton and nylon webbing. Her specialty is expressing impatience when

I become involved in dog show conversations. When finally ready to leave, I find my half of the leash empty while Sunny looks on, impossibly innocent, with six inches of leash hanging from her collar snap. The phantom dog show leash chopper has struck again.

The training collar is the most important single piece of equipment for all classes. Slip training collars come in three basic materials. The most common form is the chain collar. Chain collars tend to be thrown off over a dog's head during a jump, which is inconvenient in Open or Utility training. A smooth-coated sighthound can shed a chain collar simply by lowering his head. I used to see people with metal detectors examining the park where we trained and wondered how many of our vanished chain collars they found while searching for more interesting objects.

There are two types of nylon training collars. In the first type, the end rings are connected by a thin cord. One version of this has a braided cord that frays and become unattractive quickly. The best ones are made of parachute cord. They last forever and are decorative on a trained dog. This collar requires a very light touch because the narrow cord concentrates the correction and it is easy to overcorrect.

For training I use a collar in which the rings are connected by a nylon tape about a half inch wide. This type of collar is manufactured under the Simplicity name in England and is exported for distribution in America. It costs only a few dollars. The tape collar should be barely large enough to slide over the dog's head. It should rest in mid-neck and not slide all the way down to the shoulder. If it is too large, it will twist on itself. These collars are easy to shorten with a pair of scissors and a sewing machine. For that matter, they are easy to make. My favorite pair, which appear in many of these photos and are wider than the Simplicity version, were made from an Army surplus strap and some three-quarter-inch O-

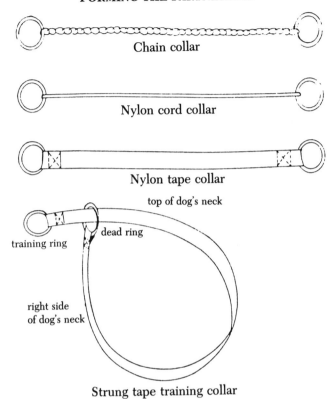

Chain collar

Nylon cord collar

Nylon tape collar

top of dog's neck

dead ring

training ring

right side
of dog's neck

Strung tape training collar

rings. The O-rings should be large enough for the trainer to hook a finger through.

All of these collars operate the same way. If a leash is attached to the training ring and pulled, the collar tightens first across the back of the dog's neck (which is why it is important to put the collar on the dog right side up). The strung collar is pictured as if you were looking at the dog head on. The quick—and it should always be quick—neck pressure is very similar to what a puppy feels when the bitch grabs it to discipline it. The idea is to startle, not strangle, the dog. If the leash is attached to the dead ring, the collar will not tighten. It then acts the same as a plain buckle collar. *Most of my Novice training is done using the dead ring so that the dog can be guided through the routines without tightening the collar.*

Active and Passive Exercises

All but one of the Novice exercises are passive in nature. A passive exercise is one in which the dog works next to the handler (within arm's reach) or one in which the dog is required *not* to do anything. Heeling and the finish are examples of the dog's working within arm's reach, hopefully. The stand, sit, and down stays are the exercises in which success means not doing anything—where not moving at all is perfection. The only action required of the dog for these exercises is that he lie down on cue. For the sit stay, the dog is already sitting in position at the start of the stay. For the stand, the dog does not even have to stand voluntarily. The handler can pick him up bodily and stack him into a stand if necessary.

The Novice exercises are passive because they were originally intended to bring a dog under the owner's control. The only exercise in Novice that requires active obedience is the recall. For this the dog is thirty feet from the handler and has to get up voluntarily and come to him. The key word to the active exercises is *voluntary*. There are two ways of teaching the active exercises. One is to use a variety of tricks and devices like long lines, throw chains, and remote electric collars, to convince the dog that the handler has the power to apply discipline from a distance of thirty feet. This is a difficult fiction to maintain. The dog keeps searching out the owner's limitations. The other approach is to teach the routines, give the dog an incentive to want to perform them, and to practice just enough to try to create the habit of doing them correctly. For this approach you never discipline the dog when he is working at a distance. The dog is not disciplined while he is working free, for the best of all possible reasons—it does not work. The owner of a simple-minded dog may gallop out and strongly correct his dog for a mistake, with a chance of improving the dog's performance. It is a rare running dog that is stupid enough to sit waiting for a correction when he knows that he is twice as fast as his owner. If an exercise is blown while free working, the answer is to go out quietly, put the dog back on leash, and do some more practice in close. Changing from working in close to working at a distance is no problem, if the dog is ready for it. Many trainers go off leash too soon and create their own problems.

As a dog progresses up through the levels of obedience, the exercise types shift from predominantly passive in Novice to almost entirely active in Utility. Trainers going from Novice to the advanced classes for the first time often either overdiscipline or start to lose control of their dogs because the trainers are unprepared for the shift in the type of exercises. For example, the exercises by class and type are:

Novice	*Active*	*Passive*
Heeling		X
Stand for Examination		X
Sit Stay		X
Down Stay		X
The Recall	X	

Open		
Heeling		X
Long Sit		X
Long Down		X
Drop on Recall	X	
Retrieve on the Flat	X	
Retrieve over the High Jump	X	
Broad Jump	X	

Utility

Long Stand		X
Signal Exercise	X	
Scent Discrimination	X	
Directed Retrieve	X	
Directed Jumping	X	

The passive exercises can be taught with a straightforward combination of praise and guidance. The active exercises require considerably more ingenuity on the part of the handler. The active exercises use motivations of food, play, and pursuit, and they are the reason that I advocate learning to play with the dog and teaching it rag games. For playtraining in the Open and Utility classes, the dog needs to know the games first.

The Exercise Order

While each new exercise is introduced, earlier ones are still being worked on. Having a number of exercises in different stages of progress keeps the dog from being bored. When trouble crops up with a familiar exercise, it can often be cured by teaching a new one. Dogs will start to revise old exercises to entertain themselves. There is no absolutely correct fixed order for introducing the exercises. There is also no reason to teach obedience strictly by class—that is, only Novice, only Open, or just Utility. Mixing routines from the different classes helps provide variety. The choice of exercises is guided by the dog's natural aptitudes. A lethargic or insecure dog may do beautiful advanced stays while being still unreliable on the more active exercises. The superlively dog will need patient work on the stays while romping through the rest of the lessons. Novice is the only class for which I have a fairly fixed lesson order. The sit and the come are taught first. These are quick to teach and they give the owner basic control of the dog. A dog that will come when it is called and sit when it is told is not likely to get into too much trouble. Because of the quick responses to these exercises, I also use them as tests for a dog's trainability. A

Any training is only as good as the quality of the praise that goes with it. The more enthusiastic the praise is, the more enthusiastic it makes the dog.

fifteen-minute test will give a good idea of a dog's mental abilities.

After teaching the sit and recall for a week or two, we add heeling and later the stand and the sit stay. Last comes the stand for examination, and the finish. And at the very end comes the down. The down is last for a definite reason: it is too easy. Most dogs would much rather down that sit. It is a good idea to work the dog for as long as possible before he finds out that there is such a thing as a down in obedience. He can still know what the word down means. Most dogs learn the meaning of down just by repetition around the house, which is fine. The dog can still believe for the first few months of obedience that the sit and stand are the only allowed positions.

A Quick Word on Praise

Praise is not a formal "Good dog!" given at the end of an exercise. Effective praise is contact with the dog whether it be hand, body, or eye contact, or all three, as in the photo. Praise is small shrieks of glee and wild wrestling matches, depending on the dog. Praise is *smiling* at the dog. Some dogs have poor eyesight but many dogs read facial expressions very well. Most of all, praise is ever present.

The Sit

In order to teach a dog to sit, I take him for a walk—a nice long, leisurely ramble in the park or a walk to the local horse show arena to watch a couple of classes. Halter classes are very much like dog shows. Every few blocks and at every street curb we try a sit, which is done by simply enfolding the dog in my arms. As shown in the photo, the handler kneels next to the dog's right side with the leash and the dog's throat in the right hand. The right thumb is hooked through the collar for better control. The left arm is placed low around the dog's rump. On the cue "Sit," the left arm sweeps in and

For the sit, the dog is enfolded in the trainer's arms. This is easily tolerated even by a shy dog.

bends the dog's rear legs while the right hand presses up and back on the neck, lifting the dog back into a sit. This pull up and back eventually becomes the standard collar aid for the sit. At first the dog is physically "sat" at the same time that he hears the word. After a half dozen tries, or when the dog has shown a tendency to bend before pressure is applied, he should be given a moment for a chance to respond before he is put into the sit. Gradually the pressure on the rear legs is decreased until a backward pull on the neck alone will sit the dog. This takes from three to four days for the dog to learn.

In teaching the sit, avoid pressing down on the dog's rump. If he is going to be shown in either breed or obedience, he had better not sit when a judge presses down on his back. Besides which, pressing down on the back is saved for another purpose. It is one of the cues for the stand. A former Army trainer once wanted to demonstrate a move with one of my dogs for which he first needed the dog in the sitting position. He pressed down on her back and told her to sit. She resisted the pressure and stood just as she had been taught. He pushed harder. She won. A dog with braced legs is almost impossible to shove into a sit. I suggested that she would not move until he took his hand off her body, to which he replied incredulously, "Don't tell me that you never pushed her down into a sit!" That was right. She never had been "sat" that way. When he let go of her, she sat on the next order, looking more than a little satisfied with herself.

One last word on the sit. If you use an arm sweep to fold a dog into the sit, and the dog resists, try again with a little more strength and a good deal more speed. Quickness is more important than strength in folding the rear legs. Sometimes the response is quick enough so that the dog ends up sitting on the handler's arm and smiling.

Some Recall Recipes

The ingredients are a pocketful of dog goodies, a lead between six to twelve feet long that will not burn your hands if you give it a good strong pull, an innocent dog, and a number of distractions to divert the dog's interest from you. Parks with ducks or squirrels, strange dogs, or anything new and different are good for recall.

For Untrained Adult Dogs. This is the second exercise that is done during that walk mentioned in the Sit section. It is a bit time-consuming, because nothing can be done while the dog's attention is on the handler. So you put the dog on a slack lead and wander around until he becomes totally engrossed in some outside distraction. Move about six feet behind the dog. Say, "Dog, come!" and give a quick, firm pull on the leash. The pull should be strong enough to start his head and shoulders turning toward you and quick enough so that by the time he turns far enough to see you there is once more slack in the lead. He sees you bending over, clapping hands, and calling him so he comes trotting over to receive a great deal of praise and a dog cracker. An experienced dog would know that the correction came from the other end of the leash even though he had not seen it done. The innocent dog simply knows that when he hears the word "come" it is not safe to be away from the handler. First the dog is startled. Then, when he turns to look for shelter, he sees the owner all smiles, encouraging him to come in for protection. Some people use different ways of startling the dog. Tossing a rock or throw chain on the ground several feet beyond the dog before calling him can have the same effect. The dog is not touched with the throw chain. The rattle as it hits the ground is the incentive. He then hears your call, turns, and there you are, his shelter. This entire method relies on having the dog be so intent on investigating something else that he does not see the handler throw the object or make the collar correction. For this reason the method does not fit into the routine of a dog-training class. It is something that the owner does alone with the dog. Do not worry if, after having the dog come three or four times, you find that he will not divert his attention or go far enough away from you to practice it again. That means the lesson is over for the day. Try it again in a few days or a week.

Recall problems are much easier to avoid than to cure. The dos and don'ts of recalls are:

DO:

1. Praise and reward the dog every time it comes when called.

2. Have a separate recall word other than "Come" just generally to call the dog at the end of a romp. Most of mine come nicely to "Cracker" as in "Hey guys, would you like a cracker?" While munching on their crackers their leashes are attached and they do not feel too unhappy about losing their freedom. They also do not connect the end of playtime with the word "Come."

3. Encourage puppies to come. Puppies have natural recall. It will never be easier to teach them to come on cue. Try to run away from them and call them for play. Carry dog biscuits. To a puppy "Come" should mean "Come and eat a dog biscuit," or "Come and play with me."

DON'T:

1. Ever call a dog to you and punish it. If you are absolutely bound to punish it, then run it down and catch it. Even then it will be learning to run from you. If a dog comes, it deserves praise no matter what it did earlier to deserve punishment. And the madder the handler is the more praise the dog deserves. He knows perfectly well from the owner's stance and tone of voice just how angry the person is. Imagine how hard it is for the dog to come in the face of his pack leader's anger.

2. Call a dog for unpleasant attention. Use the cracker bait or go and get the dog to grind its toenails or administer medication or put it in its kennel.

3. Chase a dog that will not come. Dogs love to play tag. The owner is much better off if the dogs learn to play tag by chasing the handler instead of the other way around. They should be encouraged to chase their owner from the time they are puppies.

The Problem Recall. All of the suggestions above are intended to prevent the production of dogs that recognize the "Come" and avoid obeying it whenever possible. While the come is relatively easy to teach either to a puppy or an untrained dog, it becomes much more time-consuming with a dog that has been taught to resist responding to it. There is no way to surprise that dog, and it has been fooled too many times to come out of puppy love. That brings us to the time-consuming conventional methods of first teaching the sit stay and then practicing on-leash recalls until the dog has mastered them. Then longer recalls are practiced on a twenty- to thirty-foot-long line. The line stays on the dog twice as long as the handler thinks it should. The line is inconvenient. Long lines mysteriously tie themselves into intricate knots between training sessions. There is always a temptation to try the dog just once without the line. But the only dog that is going to be worked on a line is the dog that will run from his handler. If the dog needs to be on a line in the first place, he needs to stay there until he is sound in the routine. Taking the line off a little too early can undo weeks of work, by teaching him that he has to obey only when he is on the line. There is no element of surprise in this kind of training. The handler and dog are eyeball-to-eyeball on either end of the line. If the dog moves before being called, he is taken back and sat again. If he does not get up and start in on the first command, a collar correction starts him in, and he knows full well who made that correction. There is not much fun inherent in this situation, so it takes extra praise and enthusiasm on the handler's part to keep the dog lively. The usual dog goody at the end of each recall is essential.

When working with a willing dog, you can increase the dog's pace by practicing recalls as much as twice as long as those done in the ring. Having the handler so far away makes the dog tense and makes him want to come in faster. To increase the speed of a dog that recalls slowly, it also helps to put him on the uphill end of a slight slope so that he will be coming downhill. Do not recall a slow dog uphill.

The recall is a four-part exercise. It is composed of a sit stay, the come, the sit in front, and a finish. The parts are all taught separately. When teaching the come, do not worry about the sit in front. Once the dog knows the finish, do not connect it with the recall—or the dog will quickly learn to do an automatic finish without bothering with the sit in front. A novice trainer once told me proudly that he had taught his dog the automatic finish, and I then had to explain that it is not an obedience exercise. It is a shortcut in the routine that will cost a dog from one to five points from most judges. To avoid this penalty, most of the praise and rewards for the recall are given while the dog is sitting in front of the handler to reinforce that position.

Once the recall is lengthened beyond fifteen feet, some eager dogs recall as if they were starting after a rabbit. This is beautiful as long as they are able to stop when they reach the handler. They have a tendency in the early training stages to charge on by and circle around to come back. This type of dog can be helped with a sit cue given when he is still about ten feet from the handler and in full stride. It gives him a cue on when to start to slow down. This problem is self-curing. As dogs are worked, they slow down with practice. Finally, slowness becomes the classic vice. As they become bored with the routines, they express that feeling by becoming absolute creepers. As a result, I favor the fast-working dogs and humor them. I have a current greyhound that comes in at formidable speed and, unable to quite stop, lifts her front, bounces off the handler, and back down into a sit, having used the handler as a bumperboard to stop with. Does that not sound quite like normal obedience? We have fun with it. She does lovely recalls and will be calm enough to do conventional sits by the time she is shown. When all the element of play is taken out of training, the result is a dull worker.

Heeling

Slowness as a fault is particularly evident in heeling. In terms of points earned, heeling is the most important single

A competent but unenthused heeling dog. She is in heel position but moving placidly with no dog-handler eye contact. She is a foot watcher and could be taught foot cues.

The desired heeling dog—she is animated. Her head is raised and turned to watch the handler's face. Her tail is up and wagging.

exercise that a dog can do well. The dog has to heel in all three classes and gets to do it twice in Novice (once on lead and once off lead). One of the best ways of improving heeling scores is to teach him that there are two types of heeling, competition heeling and the less formal heeling that he does just to go for walks with his owner. The problem here is that eighty percent of a dog's heeling time is spent just heeling around town, while competition heeling is the exception. As an added complication, most of my dogs' everyday heeling is done in braces. As a result the outside brace dog started leaving space for her bracemate even when heeling alone. Her position remained exact, one dog width out from my knee. Judges found this a little odd, and the habit proved very resistant to change. Now I make sure that a retired or poorer working dog goes on the outside of the brace, with the competition dog staying in close.

Virtually all green dogs begin by forging, which is pulling ahead of the handler. After sufficient training in heeling, many dogs end up by lagging behind the handler, which is not the desired goal. The desired result is a dog that moves quickly with his neck alongside the handler's knee and with the dog's head turned to look up at the handler. Really sharp dogs work as if their necks were wrapped around the handler's knee. In order to achieve this goal the following things need to be kept in mind for the heel training:

1. The leash has to be slack for heeling practice. The dog learns nothing from a tight lead. The lead snap should hang straight down below the collar. See the photos.
2. The heeling pattern should be short. It should last not more than three minutes. This enables the dog to work quickly while he is still energetic.
3. The handler should move briskly enough that the dog really has to stride out or move into a jog to keep up. The slower the handler moves, the slower the dog will move. No matter how slow the handler walks, the dog can walk

slower still. Adapting to the dog's pace makes him worse.

4. Talk to the dog at all times, encouraging him to stay alongside.

5. The correction for a forging dog is not a pull back on the collar. It is a verbal caution, "Easy puppy, back here," and if that does not produce a response, the correction is a change of direction, either a right turn or an about turn with a quick, light tug on the collar and a verbal, "Oops, get up here" to help him catch up.

6. Praise the dog all the time he is heeling, not just at the sits. Pet his head and rumple his ears. Give him a reason to want to stay close to you.

7. In order to heel well, the dog has to *want* to stay with the handler. It is not a punishment-oriented exercise, although it is often taught as one. Leash corrections in heeling should be light and kept to a minimum. From the dog's point of view, he should think he accidentally ran into the end of the leash because he was not concentrating and missed a turn. Particularly, do not continually correct a lagging dog. He can be encouraged to keep up, but being yanked up will have no lasting effect. It simply makes him hate heeling and lag all the more.

8. Do not be too eager to take the leash off. The leash is a guide that can be used to help perfect the most experienced dog. If a dog is worked up to a high level of competency on leash, he may well not care when it is removed.

The first step in going leashless is to leave the leash on the dog and drape the end across the handler's chest and over the right shoulder. This leaves the hands free, but the leash is easy to reach if it is needed. If the leash goes untouched the next step is adding the light line. The funky-looking necklace visible on the handler in some of these photos is a light line—two feet of nylon cord with a light snap on one end and a wrist loop on the other. These lines are sold for show leads at

The proper heeling dog is alert even when he is just sitting at heel.

It takes a dog some time to stand up and start heeling. This often creates a lag in the first few heeling steps, where the dog is too far behind the handler. Do NOT pull on a lagging dog to make it move faster. You just teach it to hate heeling.

West Coast shows. To use the light line, attach both leash and line to the collar ring. Do a very short heeling pattern to divert the dog's attention. Conspicuously remove the leash and drop it. Continue heeling. With luck and a well-trained dog, the line will not be used. If the dog decides to smell the ground or wander off, he receives a single light line correction, which should surprise him considerably. Praise him. Do a short heel and stop. Put him back on leash and change to a different exercise. As soon as that first correction is made, the dog is going to watch to see how it was done. The first

*The easy way to persuade a dog to start out fast is simple bribery.
A dog biscuit, which is waved in front of his nose and which he is
allowed to catch if he hurries, will speed up most dogs. A few weeks
of mild bribery will teach the dog to start quickly, and then the
reward can be given occasionally to reinforce the habit.*

correction in each session with a light line is the only one that does any good. After that he is only learning to watch for the line. For the dog that is an expert at spotting light lines, clear fishing line is sometimes used although it is hard on the trainer's hands.

Really good heeling is virtually a dance form in which the dog and handler are partners. The handler is leading and giving both the "heel" cue and many subtle body cues that can help the dog. Bending very slightly at the knees just before a halt can prepare the dog for it. Turning the left foot in the direction of a turn for a step before the turn is made will forewarn dogs that carry their heads low enough to see the handler's feet. The greatest help a dog can have is for the handler to move smoothly and not go from normal speed to fast in a single step. A military pivot will leave the best dog behind. In every turn except the left turn, the dog has much farther to walk than the handler does. If the handler walks with quick little steps through a small radius turn instead of performing a sharp pivot then the dog has a chance to stay in step. There are many possible heeling variations that can be used to perfect the dog but are *never seen* in the show ring. They are only limited by the trainer's imagination. Here are a few:

1. *The Step Off:* While heeling in a straight line, the handler takes one giant step to the right, away from the dog. This leaves about two feet of space between them, with both still headed in the original direction. The handler keeps walking while praising and calling the dog. This exercise is a pure praise incentive. The dog will scuttle to cross over and close the gap. He learns to work at staying close and to watch for unusual moves.

2. *The U-turn:* This variation is an about-turn done toward the dog. It can be either two left turns linked or a short semicircle. The latter is the same as the inside turn of the figure eight. Any variation to practice the figure eight is

helpful. The eight is a deadly dull exercise because it is always done the same way. Most judges even call the two required halts at the same place, midway between the posts. In practice matches we do cloverleafs that include the judge as part of the pattern. In straight heeling, a serpentine pattern can provide practice for the inside and outside turns of the figure eight. Jogging around the pattern helps keep the dog awake. Most dogs turn into robots on the eight. We once had a post steward (she was also the judge's wife) who came out in a full-length rabbit-fur coat. Tiger's eyes lit up as this five-foot rabbit approached. On the second time around I ended up on the far end of the figure while my Greyhound was still moving leisurely and longingly around the judge's wife. The second halt was called, and I stopped facing Tiger and his bunny. He gave a last wistful sniff, left her, and completed the other half of the figure eight to come back into heel position. Most dogs can do the figure eight in their sleep. Many appear to.

3. *The Pivot:* This variation works beautifully in Advanced Novice to sharpen up heeling. It is actually the beginning of the directed retrieve exercise in Utility. Starting out at heel, the dog is given the heel cue and the handler pivots an eighth of a turn to the right. The dog is called, guided with the leash, and told to "Sit straight" to get him into the new heel position. When he has mastered the pivot to the right, the left pivot is introduced, which is more difficult for the dog. Put tension in the leash so he cannot move forward. Give the heel cue and turn toward the dog. Nudge him in the shoulder with your left knee to start him backing around. If his rump swings out from the heel position instead of toward it, guide his hip with your left hand. The first turns to the left should be very small. If he moves and sits crooked at first, praise him and then take a step forward and tell him to sit straight. Eventually he will

be able to back into a straight sit, but that is asking too much of a dog that is just learning to pivot. The pivots in both directions teach the dog to adjust his position to stay at heel, and they teach him the difference between crooked sits and straight sits. Incidentally, the command "Sit straight" always applies to a sit at heel. To straighten up a dog that is crooked after a recall the cue is "Front," or "Come front." It means to sit straight facing the handler. (The handler may think the dog is sitting crooked in either case but to the dog these are two different exercises.)

4. *The Come to Heel:* The dog is left on a sit stay. The handler takes several steps, stops, and calls, "Heel" with his back to the dog. The first few times a great deal of encouragement is in order, as the dog will be confused. He is not accustomed to looking at the handler's back on any exercise except a sit stay. This move can be varied by adding a turn to either side so that the handler's shoulder is toward the dog when he is called to heel. In no case is the handler more than eight feet from the dog, and the move is never done facing the dog or he will confuse it with the recall. The come to heel is another way of showing the dog the meaning of the heel position. I've often seen dogs at trials that were totally unable to find the heel position from anywhere beside or behind the handler. This variation is good practice for the ambidextrous dog that at first will heel on either the left or right side. Some novice dogs understand the meaning of heel before that of left and right. Keep shifting the dog gently to the left side and he will eventually stay there. Do not correct a dog for heeling on the right side. From the dog's viewpoint he would have been corrected for trying to heel.

The Sit Stay

The key to the sit stay is not to hurry it, but to make slow steady progress with each practice session. With the dog in a sit at the heel position for the first stay, the handler steps around in front of the dog. With each practice the distance is increased, the handler moving back until the end of the leash is reached. If the dog is very steady, you simply drop the leash on the ground and gradually continue to increase the distance. If there is any chance of his breaking, lay a long line out ahead of time between where he is going to sit and where you are going to stand. Clip it to his collar as you sit him for the stay. If you unreel the long line while walking away from him it is too conspicuous. He knows exactly what you are doing. Both the long line and the light line should be unnoticed by the dog.

First sit the dog. The "Stay" cue is given without the dog's name. Most cues are preceded by the dog's name as in, "Sunny, heel." A well-trained dog will start to move whenever it hears its name. If I were to say "Sunny, stay," she would be halfway up out of the sit before she ever heard the "stay." So the stay is given by itself. A secondary cue involves taking the first heeling step with the left foot and the first step out from a stay with the right foot. There are dogs that work the stays and heeling on foot cues alone. Never having had much luck at quickly and consistently telling left from right myself, I do not use this cue. Confusing left and right seems to be a family trait. My sister used to lead an equestrian drill team with LEFT written on the back of her left hand and RIGHT written on the back of her right hand. I have occasionally contemplated doing the same thing in the obedience ring.

When you are ready to step away from the dog (starting with the right foot), give the stay cue and hand signal. The stay hand signal is the palm of either open hand swung down just short of the dog's nose. In first teaching the stay, we cheat and touch the nose gently. At the same time we step around to face the dog. He will most likely be staying, since, in order to move, he would have had to push through the hand signal. The stay is repeated and the dog is steadied with a hand on the shoulder. The trainer walks around behind the dog to come back to heel. The dog is held still for a moment and then released from the exercise and praised. The collar correction is the same quick pull up and back that is the sit correction, followed immediately by praise as he comes into position. The rest of the sit stay is just a matter of slowly increasing the time of the sit and the distance between the dog and handler.

When the dog is steady on the sit stay for a three-minute period at a distance of thirty feet, it is time to find other dogs to practice with. Nothing in everyday life prepares a dog for a sit stay as part of a fifteen-dog lineup. Try to avoid practicing with a Novice class that is just starting sit stays. At first you do not need strange dogs bolting past your beginner, nor do you need harried owners leaping back to correct their dogs. Such activity is rather more distraction than there will be at a normal trial. The idea is to find a place where the dog can succeed and gain confidence, not fail and be disciplined. The best company to start with is a group of experienced Open B dogs that are practicing the out-of-sight stays. By the time a dog reaches Open B it may scratch or eat grass or fall asleep in the stays, but it is not likely to get up and leave the ring. The Open B lineup is a peaceful place to practice Novice in-sight sits, and the handlers will often welcome a Novice to help fill out the line. They will be practicing a three-minute sit and a five-minute down. The three-minute sit is good practice for a Novice dog. The five minutes is a bit too long, but you can go back and quietly break him out of it at the three-minute mark. If an Open B lineup is not available, then the practice sessions toward the middle of a Novice class are acceptable, after the rowdier dogs have settled down some-what. The first time the dog is worked with company, have a long line on him no matter how reliable he has been in the past. He still has to demonstrate his steadiness in the presence of strange dogs. The end of the lineup is the least vulnerable position when you are working with a group of green Novice dogs. While the rest of the class does one sit stay and one down stay, do a pair of sits. The down is not introduced until the sits are very stable.

The Stand for Examination ·

One of the most durable myths of obedience is that training will ruin a breed dog for the show ring because the dog learns to sit. No matter how many Champion-Utility dogs there are, the fallacy dies hard. The problem with a dog that sits in the ring is not that he has been taught to sit but that he has not been taught to stand properly. It is an easy mistake to make because the basic sit can be taught in a couple of days while the basic stand takes several weeks. A sitting dog is well settled into position while a standing dog is ready to move in any direction. And while a command of "Lie down and stay there" makes sense to the dog—he is supposed to get comfortable and wait for his owner—a command of "Stand up and stay there" must seem totally irrational to him. An immobilized dog does not stand. After a while he either sits or lies down to relax. However, to get back to the stand, start with one sitting dog. His collar should be snug enough so that it will not slide off easily over his head. Hook your right thumb under the collar for control. Slide your left hand under the dog in front of the stifle, with the palm of the hand down. This is important. You will be lifting with the back of the hand against the dog. If the dog is uncooperative at first, it is easy to accidentally clench that hand. If the palm is turned toward the dog, you will have just grabbed a handful of dog. Many dogs, and especially male dogs, justifiably object to being pinched. So the hand stays open and the palm down. Give the stand cue, pulling forward on the collar and lifting with the back of the left hand. Once the dog is up, his rear feet can be stacked into a comfortable

The dog is lifted into the stand stay with the back of the trainer's hand.

position. Help him to hold the stand for a few moments. With each practice, the time for the stand is increased even more slowly than it was for the sit stay. As the stand becomes steady, start to go over the dog with your left hand. This works up from just scratching his belly to fussing with his feet and tail, running a hand down his back and applying pressure to teach the dog to resist it. The next stage is to release the collar and gradually work your way around the dog, doing a breed type of examination which is much more thorough than the token obedience version of a hand run down the back. By this time the dog should be quite secure on the stand and, if he knows the sit stay, he is ready for the final move. You stand the dog, press down along his back, give him a "Stay" cue and a hand signal just as if it were a sit stay, and walk out in front of the dog. You and he stare at each other for a few minutes and you then circle around behind him to the heel position. The dog is apt to move as you come to heel or to try to sit when he realizes that you are at heel, so run a hand down his back and maintain hand contact to keep him standing, at first. Then taper off the hand contact until he will hold the stand without it.

For the well-socialized dog, the examination is an insignificant part of the routine. First practice examinations yourself, playing the part of both the handler and the judge. When the dog is good at it with you, try having someone else do the examination. Very friendly dogs will be steadier when examined by a stranger. If the dog greets the examiner with leaps of joy, stay in close for a few attempts until the dog settles down.

For the shy dog the examination is more complicated. Start with an examiner known to the dog and practice with the dog in the sitting position. The dog is more likely to hold a sit than a stand. We would not want to discipline the dog for faults in the stand while trying to build his confidence in the examination. Stay close to the dog for reassurance. If he will take food, have the examiner bait him. Do not sympathize with the dog's fears. If he is encouraged to do so, he will hide behind his owner for the rest of his life. Dogs are sensitive to a slightly disparaging tone of voice, as in, "Hold still, silly. What is this nonsense?" Above all, do not sound worried or irritated. If the owner is worried, why should the dog be calm? When the dog can manage an examination at the sit, move him into the stand and keep practicing with the owner alongside. The last step is for the owner to move away from the dog. (All of this work is done on leash.) If the shy dog once bolts away from an exam, it will take a great deal of work to steady him again. The examiner should be told in advance to back off quickly should the dog start to panic.

The handler is allowed to stack the dog for the stand. The dog should be left in a comfortable, balanced position, with the hind feet not extended too far back. The most common single fault of Novice handlers in the stand is to give the stay cue while still touching the dog with one hand. The dog is supposed to be standing free when he is told to stay. The second most common error is for the handler to go farther than six feet in front of the dog. Six feet should be easy to judge. It means standing one leash length in front of the dog's nose.

The Down Stay

This is almost a self-teaching exercise. If the dog is doing good sit stays he will have little trouble with the stay part of the routine. Most dogs half learn the down around the house with "Go lie down in the corner," or "Get down" in the car. Since it is the last Novice exercise taught and it does not take long, I have occasionally arrived at practice matches before realizing that I had not yet bothered to teach that dog the down.

If the dog is really unaware of the meaning of the word, a couple of days of physical demonstration are needed, as for the sit. In this case, sit the dog and kneel next to him. Slide an arm across his shoulders and hold a foreleg in each hand, grasping the forelegs just below the elbow. You can now lay him down gently on the "Down" cue by leaning a little weight on his shoulders, and lifting and stretching his forelegs out in front of him. He will find himself lying in the sphinx position with his body in a straight line centered on his breastbone. This is a good position for grass rings. Most sighthounds, having no body padding and preferring soft beds, are going to object to lying down on concrete. If the handler persists, the dog will accept hard surfaces, and in an area with predominantly indoor shows he will have to. There is a risk that dogs with thin skin and prominent bones will develop pressure sores where the bones of the hock or elbow will wear through the skin. I prefer not to lie on concrete myself and do not ask my dogs to practice on it. They have put up with enough of my whims not to have to be uncomfortable. Dogs differ from each other in their ability to tolerate hard surfaces. Dogs have a problem that people do not have. When a person sits he is resting on a well padded posterior. When a dog sits, some of the heavy-bodied overweight dogs may be resting on their rumps but long-legged dogs are not really sitting at all. Their rumps never touch the ground. They actually squat on their hocks (which are analogous to our heels). This means that all their weight is bearing along their foot from the hock down to the toes. Some dogs have dense fur below the hock which protects them from the pressure. I used to have to clip this area on my collie to give him the desired tidy-footed appearance. Dogs with fine skin and short hair have little protection between the prominent hock bones and the pavement. These dogs should not be worked on pavement unless rubber matting or carpet is provided in the rings. Ideally these dogs should be shown in grass rings.

The same dogs who are subject to pressure problems in the sitting position will have similar problems in the long down unless you have them lie flat on their sides. If a prominent-boned, fine-coated dog is placed in a sphinx position down on pavement, then the pain on his brisket and elbows will force him to move. If you are tempted to punish him for moving, then try a simple exercise instead. Wear shorts and a short-sleeved shirt and take off your shoes and socks. Find some nice rough asphalt and do a one minute sit; hunker down on your heels for a minute. You may find it a bit uncomfortable. After that, try a sphinx position down. From a kneeling position you reach out in front and rest your forearms on the pavement with the elbows a foot apart and the wrists together. Do not try this if you have back problems. Rest half of your weight on your arms and stay there for three or five minutes, depending on whether you are practicing the Novice long down or the Open long down. You probably will not make the time limit. Do your elbows hurt? You bet your dumbbell, they hurt. That is because your weight is concentrated on your poorly-padded knees and elbows. This pressure point problem is the same as that faced by the poorly-padded types of dogs. It is the reason that some breeds tolerate poor ring surfaces less well than other breeds do. When it comes to ring surfaces, all dogs are not equal. Some dogs are penalized much more heavily by them than others.

After you have tried the long down in the sphinx position, roll over on your back and lie out flat. You will find it a great improvement because your weight is distributed over the broadest part of your body. This is the equivalent of having the dog lie flat on his side on a hard surface. If you leave a pressure-point-problem dog on a down in the sphinx position on a paved surface, then you should expect him to move. Punishment is not the solution to this. Relieving the pain is the solution.

When first teaching any word to a dog, I repeat it often to familiarize the dog with the sound and help him to recognize it. Once the dog understands the word and the action it is related to, repetition only teaches the dog to wait to hear it again. So after that the dog hears only one cue. Once the dog connects the word "Down" with being down, the downward pressure on the shoulder is replaced by a downward pull on the collar. Pointing at the ground or patting it will help the beginner go down. I do not emphasize much authority when teaching the down because of the dogs' tendency to drop voluntarily. Once dogs discover that they are allowed to lie down in obedience, they start lying down all over the place, particularly as the handler walks away for a recall or suffers through a long sit. I sometimes wondered if there was any circumstance under which Sunny would not lie down. At the start of a figure eight the judge asked routinely if I was ready. I agreed. He said, "No, you are not. Look at your dog." I looked to find that Sunny had silently snuggled down into three inches of soaking wet grass. It is a good idea to check the dog to see if you are both ready. On Sunny's first Open leg, the judge asked that she be stood for measuring. "Sunny, stand." Sunny lay down deliberately. The judge said, "If I measure her that way she will only have to jump eighteen inches instead of thirty-six."

With practice, the dog eventually goes down on the single cue without the handler's needing to lean over or point. If you find yourself at a trial with a dog whose down you are not sure of, there are several things that can help. Drop the dog outside the ring a few times to refresh his memory. Inside the ring, if it is a question of passing or failing, help the dog. Repeat the command if necessary. Go ahead and lean and point. If you can get the dog down without his active resistance, he can still qualify if he holds the down. The long down is not a test of how well the dog lies down. It is a test of how well he stays down.

The Finish

There are four types of finishes (we illustrated the flip in the first chapter). I do not use the military finish, as a long-bodied dog often does not go far enough past the handler to give himself room to turn and sit straight. To teach the swing finish, first teach the dog the left-hand heeling pivot (discussed earlier in the heeling section). The swing finish is a solo left-hand pivot by the dog with the handler standing still. Once the dog has the pivot well learned, put him in a front sit. Give him the heel cue and swing your shoulders to the left as if starting a pivot. See if he will swing to heel. Guide him with the leash and keep him moving until he is all the way around at heel. This is one place where a little nagging helps.

The easiest finish to teach the inexperienced dog is the conventional one. The dog walks a circle around the handler and sits. Many books and trainers advocate sharp leash pulls and even throwing the dog behind the handler for this move. Do not do it. Have faith. The dog will move with no more than gentle guidance. Most harsh methods are the result of a trainer's trying to take shortcuts. There are no shortcuts to a good obedience dog. First, wrap the leash behind your body from right to left and hold it in the left hand. Drape it low enough so that you can step back with your right leg to push against the leash and tighten the collar. The dog is sitting facing you. Give him the heel cue. Call him and back up. If he is up and coming toward you, do not tighten the leash. If he is still sitting, step back against it and tug on his collar. When he is up and moving, you change direction and move forward. This puts him behind you. Reeling in some more leash will turn him and bring him up on your left side to heel.

The conventional finish eventually outlives its usefulness. Experienced dogs may increase the diameter of their circle to preposterous degrees. When Sunny first introduced this move, she turned on the heel cue and walked ten feet to the side. It looked as if she were leaving the ring, which she had never done before. I was about to call her when she made another right-angle turn and headed behind me. Suddenly it was clear. She was doing a finish that was a square measuring ten feet on each side. After two more turns she did a nice straight sit at heel. The judge looked a little puzzled. We went home and taught her the swing finish, which is the only solution for the dog that has started to broaden the conventional finish.

The Flip Recipe

Since I used the flip as a pictured example, it is only fair to explain how it is taught, to show how playtraining guidance works. To begin with, the flip is not an appropriate exercise

The following (pages 97–99) five photos show the easiest finish to teach. Left: Here the dog, who is very new to training, is being praised to get him to hold his front-sit position. Right: With a little encouragement and eye contact he is steady on the front sit and ready to start the finish.

for all dogs. The first necessary ingredient is an outgoing dog that is a rather eager bouncer. At about the age of four months, most of my dogs are taught to keep all four feet on the ground. The prospective flip dog is taught instead that she can leap up and down all she wants but if she reaches out to tap a person on the chest the response will be a disgusted "Ick" or other uncomplimentary word. Dogs learn quite quickly to keep the front feet tucked in and just bounce.

Unfortunately, this is not absolutely reliable. Every once in a while a quick foot will reach you. If you are not prepared with some old clothes, and are not able to tolerate an occasional tap, then forget the flip and teach a conventional finish. If the occasional muddy foot does not discourage you, as soon as the dog knows the sit command he can start on the flip. Trip started the game at five months of age.

First you roughhouse with the dog for a few moments so that he wants to jump up. Bring him on leash into the sit position. Step around in front so that you are facing him. He does not have to know "Stay" for this, as you can steady him with a hand on his neck or shoulder while you move in front.

Left to Right: The handler gives the heel cue and steps across in front of the dog so that her left foot is next to the dog's right side. To avoid being left behind, the dog gets up and starts to turn.

The handler guides him with the leash as he turns behind her and comes back to heel position.

Having reached heel position he gets both praise and an ear scratch. This is the most natural finish method and seems the easiest for the dog to understand.

Talk to him. The monologue at this point goes something like this, "Waaait. Eeasy, dog. All right, are you ready?" At this point, with luck, he is watching you, because you have just been playing with him and he wants to play again. What follows will be hard for dignified trainers, but you then give the cue with a small squeal of glee and a little bound in the air. You can flap your arms or clap your hands, whatever the dog thinks is fun. If he accepts your game, he will give a small leap in place for which you praise him enormously, and you wrestle with him for a few seconds so he does really get to play. Do it twice more and quit for the day. The dog should always want to do more leaps than he has the chance to do.

Three or four days later try it again. When he is well into the game after a few weeks, and you have both his attention and a consistent bound in place, add the second part.

After the bound in place, praise him verbally while taking a couple of steps backward and calling him, if necessary, to get him moving briskly toward you. You guide him with the leash so he will pass on your left side. When his head is close to your knee, change direction; that is, stop backing up and step forward. As his head comes past your knee, call him and guide him with the leash to turn toward you. At this point you are walking forward past his tail and he is turning and trying to catch up to you, coming up on your left side to heel position. Do not make him sit at that position. Praise him when he gets there. Then tell him to sit. Now is when he gets his main praise, body and eye contact, and another chance to play with the handler. The leash guidance is only guidance and not a snap or a correction. It gently shows him which way to move. What he is doing is a leap in place followed by a swing finish. After he plays the game for a month or two, you will see him gradually start to swing while airborne. At first he will just swing a little bit to your left and finish the rest of it on the ground, but as the habit grows stronger and he gets both the range and the feel of it, the whole exercise will be done above the ground. You may think that six months is a long time to teach an obedience exercise. It is. But it is not a long time to play a fun game. At the time the photos were taken Trip had been doing the flip for nine months, and the total elapsed training time on it was about six hours done in three-minute sessions.

One word of caution: Keep your chin up! Once the dog is doing the leap, resist the temptation to lean over, look down at him, and give the command. The dog does not check to be sure that everything above him is clear before he leaps. He tucks his nose down and leads with the top of his head. He is rising fast and the top of his head is very hard. Try to avoid it.

Oops, Missed! It takes a dog that is learning the flip some time to perfect its aim. The first flip of each day is apt to be somewhat off target as the dog warms up. Trip is not usually this far off.

The cue word should be something other than "Heel," as the dog will bounce a little whenever he hears the finish cue. Trip was taught to finish to "Heel," and as a result she now does regular heeling on hand signals to avoid little extra leaps in the ring.

"HAPPINESS IS A WELL-TRAINED DOG."

Motto of the Los Padres Obedience Club

The Open Class Exercises

The Disaster Class

Some of the dogs who breezed easily through Novice will also succeed in Open A. Most dog-handler teams, however, have a problem with Open A. At an average obedience trial over sixty percent of the Novice dogs will qualify, while a passing rate of twenty-five percent is considered normal for the Open A class. This percentage is not due to any impossibility in the class exercises. Once the dogs are experienced in Open A the success rate in Open B rises above fifty percent. What makes Open A the disaster class is that many inexperienced handlers assume it is simply an extension of Novice. The Open exercises are different in kind from the Novice exercises. The Novice exercises are designed to display control of the dog; they are passive exercises requiring simply that the dog obey. The Open and Utility classes introduce exercises in which the dog has to act on his own initiative at a distance from his handler. It is at this point that the willingness of the dog to participate in the sport is going

103

to show up. It is also at this point that the trainer's ingenuity is called upon to provide the dog with both more inventive instruction and positive incentives to perform.

Why teach Open? I have a special affection for the Open class. It is in this class that many dogs and owners first begin to work toward partnership and the goal of the willing dog. Novice is too easy to teach. It is so easy that it can be and often is taught through conventional adversary training methods. Because the Novice exercises are passive in nature, they work reasonably well even with the discipline-oriented techniques. Novice has never been my favorite class since, as usually taught, it acts as a depressant on the dogs. My interest in Novice was reawakened when I tried teaching it by the same methods used for Open and Utility: that is, positive incentive training.

If your dog learned Novice by positive reinforcement methods, we just continue that system for the next two classes. If he was taught previously by adversary methods, this is the time to evaluate training methods. The higher you train in the class levels the more important it becomes to have the dog's good will and willing cooperation. These are obtained by praising the dog and helping him to succeed in the exercises so that he earns still more praise. Most dogs can be turned into "praise junkies." They will work just as hard to obtain their emotional reward as for any other incentive. For the dog of cool temperament, food or mock prey may be used to provide added incentives.

The problem with negative reinforcements is that they inhibit a dog's ability to make independent choices, to act on his own initiative. Fear created by previous punishments paralyzes the dog's mind and hinders his performance. This is not to say that we will never use negative reinforcement on a dog, but that we try to minimize negative incentives and diminish them toward zero while providing the maximum possible creative encouragement.

The Essential Pretraining

Due Warning—This is the most important section in this book.

Pretraining is a series of games that the dog and owner play before formal training for a given exercise begins. The games familiarize the dog with many of the actions that he will be called upon to use in later training. When a dog learns an exercise, he actually has to learn two different things. First he has to learn technically how to perform the action, whether that is how to jump a fence or how to pick a dumbbell up from the ground. This action can best be learned in pretraining games. Secondly, he has to learn to perform the routine on cue. This second part is the formal training. In it he learns to perform the actions—which he has already been doing in play—upon cue from his owner. There is no reason to teach both of these things at the same time. Attempts to do so only confuse the dog. If, on the other hand, the pretraining has been done patiently and thoroughly, the formal training follows easily and pleasantly.

Pretraining is both more important and of longer duration than the formal training. The games should be played for at least a couple of months before formal training is started. The pretraining games are the most important help I can give you.

Obedience Obstacles

The first major piece of equipment needed for Open obedience training (other than the dog) is a set of portable jumps, which consists of one high jump and one broad jump (see photo) and, later on, one bar jump for Utility. Standard-sized jumps used in obedience trials are five feet wide. No one needs jumps this size unless the jumps are going to take up permanent residence in the backyard or be transported by van. What is needed is lightweight jumps between 42″ and 48″ wide that will fit into a car trunk. Jumps have been part of my trunk equipment for years. Portable jumps are commercially available from mail order companies.

The Erratic Dumbbell

The dumbbell is a sly and devious beast. Go to any obedience trial and watch for its tricks. See the middle-aged lady heave it clear out of the ring twice in a row as if she were practicing for the Olympic javelin team. See the polite gentleman judge bring it back to her each time, while the dog looks on in some confusion and decides that if the judge will bring the darn thing back there is no point in having a mere dog retrieve it. See the dumbbell thrown neatly in good position only to have it bounce fifteen feet to the side. The

Beginning jumps are set narrow for the broad jump (shown) and short for the high jump.

path of a bouncing dumbbell is about as predictable as that of
a fumbled football in a Super Bowl game.

First we need control over the dumbbell. This is obtained
by practicing with it *without the dog*. It is easier to
concentrate on one thing at a time.

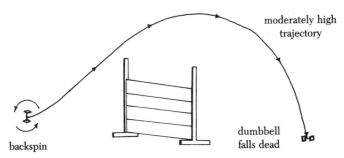

moderately high
trajectory

backspin

dumbbell
falls dead

For grass and carpet

The Throw For Grass. In order to keep a dumbbell from
rolling from its landing position, try throwing it with a
moderately high trajectory so that it is falling almost ver-
tically when it lands. The addition of a backspin will keep it
from rolling away from the jump. In order to apply a
backspin, hold the dumbbell by its upper end with your hand
down at your side. With the arm staying down, flex your
wrist forward ninety degrees so the dumbbell comes to the
horizontal position. Do it again and release the dumbbell. It
should have a backspin. This same flip of the wrist, while
using the arm to throw the dumbbell, will release it with a
backspin.

The Throw for Floors and Pavement. When faced with a
very smooth, hard surface on which the dumbbell is going to
roll no matter how it is thrown, all that can be done is to try
to control the roll. This is achieved by using a throw that you
know will roll after impact, a throw with a flat trajectory and
no spin—this is the kind of throw that causes nervous

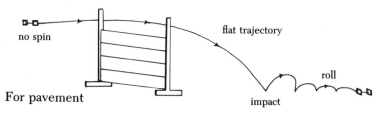

exhibitors to throw the dumbbell clear out of the ring. Under the pressure of competition they forget their own strength. In order to make use of this throw, you should aim for a point short of where you want the dumbbell to come to rest, leaving space for the roll to take it to the desired place.

Pretraining Games—The Retrieve

The Dumbbell as a Play Toy. There is no reason that a dog's first sight of a wooden dumbbell should come at a training session. Recently a trainer asked why his dog refused to pick up a dumbbell although he would willingly carry rubber chew toys. Getting a sudden mental image of the puppy pen at home with its litter of Cressite rubber toys and two well-chewed wooden dumbbells, I suggested leaving a spare dumbbell in the run for the dog to play with. Three weeks later the report came back that the dog now would not only pick up the dumbbell but would defend it in tug-of-war games with its kennelmates. There is no reason for a dog to think dumbbells are for obedience only. They make fine toys. Their main drawback is that they are a little noisy when played with on cement at two in the morning, but you can go back to sleep reciting, "C.D.X., here we come."

The Rag Game. This is the ultimate multipurpose pretraining game. It will be used for the retrieve, the broad jump, the go away, the directed retrieve, and, if you care to show in Mexico, for the seek back. (In Mexico the seek back is used in place of the directed retrieve.) The game itself is simple. You

People often wistfully complain that their dogs display little interest in either food or in rag games. There are few dogs that bait well naturally or are born rag dogs. Both traits are developed through practice. You teach a dog to bait well for food by hand feeding him frequently. You teach a dog to be a good rag dog by playing with him. This is an eight-week-old puppy playing with a sock on a string and showing good rag dog potential.

The adult dog is enjoying a game of tug-of-war and becoming a good rag dog without knowing it.

A good example of the desired end result—a properly fanatic rag dog having fun.

need a large supply of expendable soft strong rags. Small or torn towels and athletic socks are ideal. Tee shirts with knots in them work beautifully. Men's underwear works pretty well but sometimes the onlookers do not seem to understand. The game is simply to take the dog out to a safe open area and play keep away, tug-of-war, and catch with the dog. The dog is always allowed to win and to tear at the rag and kill it. But the dog is never allowed to have the rag for as long as it wishes. The rag remains an object of avid interest. After thinking that using the rag game to motivate dogs for obedience was an original idea, I spent a dog-show dinner in the company of a police officer who trains drug detection dogs. Try guessing what motivates a dog to work for long periods of time searching out small concealed amounts of illegal drugs. Is it the pungent whiff of marijuana or a desire for the handler's approval? No. The first prerequisite for a drug-detection dog in training is that it learn to be an absolutely fanatic rag dog. What the dog is actually hunting is a piece of towel which he is allowed to play with and kill at the end of the search. After the dog has killed many towels in practice and is sufficiently motivated, his formal training starts. He learns that his beloved towel can be found wherever he smells drugs. Since most drug dealers do not pack a towel in with their shipments, the handler on a real search carries a pice of towel to give the dog at the end of a successful hunt. This is a beautiful instance of rag motivation put to practical use.

From the rag game the dog learns to run to a target, pick

The dog on the left is holding a conventional broad dowel dumbbell. It prevents him from closing his mouth comfortably. The dog on the right is more happily holding a dumbbell with a narrow dowel.

an object up from the ground, and follow something white
that his owner throws. He learns that all of this is fun. In the
meantime, at home he will be learning that dumbbells are
just hard play toys. Once the dog has mastered the pretraining play, which may take several months, teaching the
retrieve is going to be fairly simple. Most importantly, the
dog is not corrected or punished for anything he does up to
this point. It is all fun. If he does not want to play today, he
will play tomorrow. Be patient. When the dog is a keen rag
dog and will voluntarily play with a dumbbell, he is ready to
start on the formal training.

The Sighthound Dumbbell. The A.K.C. specifies that the
dumbbell be of hardwood, be a single piece, and be in
proportion to the dog's size. Most dumbbells used in
competition, including mine, are not made in a single piece.
They are made from a center dowel with the ends set on and
glued. Many of the dumbbells are not hardwood. I was
surprised to find that some of the larger ones weight as little
as if they were made of balsa wood. These have a tendency to
break when thrown. The light weight is sought because the
average dog is more willing to lift a light object than a heavy
one.

Sighthounds have some special requirement when it comes
to dumbbell selection. If the ends of the dumbbell are close
together, with a short dowel, a sighthound with his narrow

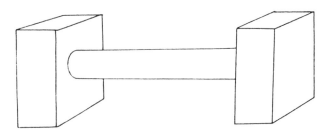

Standard dumbbell
For short-muzzled, broad-jawed dogs

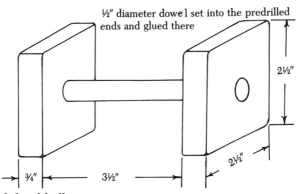

½" diameter dowel set into the predrilled ends and glued there

2½"

¾"   3½"   2½"

Sighthound dumbbell
For dogs with lòng tapered muzzles

jaw has a better chance of grasping the dowel in the center, instead of draping it unbalanced out of the corner of his mouth. If the dumbbell ends are tall and narrow, their height will raise the dowel, making it easier for the dog to grasp without needing to scrape his chin on the ground. The narrowness of the ends decreases the total weight of the dumbbell, making the dog more willing to carry it. The dowel should be half the diameter of those on conventional shepherd-style dumbbells. In the photo the red bitch is holding a dumbbell proportioned for sighthounds. The brindle dog is holding a conventional dumbbell, and he is unable to close his mouth comfortably because of the large size of the dowel.

Now for the tough question. Someone is bound to ask where sighthound dumbbells can be bought. Mine were obtained from an obedience club that manufactured them for their classes. They are finally becoming available from obedience mail order suppliers. Many obedience clubs have a member who, for the sake of the sport, has a little sideline in manufactured obedience equipment. One thing obedience dogs test is the owner's scavenging ability. It particularly helps to have a family member who does a little woodworking.

The illustrated dumbbell is sized for medium-sized sighthounds: Afghan Hounds, Greyhounds, Ibizans, Pharoahs, Salukis, and small Borzoi. It will also work well for Collies, Dobermans and other medium-sized pointed-nosed dogs. Whippets will need a dumbbell two thirds of the size shown, while Scottish Deerhounds and Irish Wolfhounds will need one half again or twice as large as the example. Italian Greyhounds, of course, will need a miniature version, keeping in mind the basic principles of using a very narrow dowel and relatively tall but narrow end pieces.

Dumbbells made to the sighthound pattern must be hardwood for strength, due to the thinness of the parts. I have never broken a hardwood dumbbell. It is utterly dismaying to see someone blow a leg on his dog's C.D.X. because of a broken dumbbell. It happened to a fine working Afghan Hound who was doing beautifully until her dumbbell landed in two pieces on the far side of the high jump. If this should ever happen to you, look quickly at the judge and ask to send the dog anyway. The chances are excellent that the dog will bring back half the dumbbell, and most judges will consider that as passing.

Dogs seldom bring back a strange dumbbell. I train with a pair of dumbbells interchangeably and carry the extra one along to shows, having learned the hard way. Just as we went into Open B, we were blithely informed by the lady with the country's top German Shepherd that she had borrowed our dumbbell, having left hers in the car. Her dog had performed fine with the strange dumbbell, but was Tiger about to bring me a dumbbell covered with strange German Shepherd spit? Not likely. He kept looking for his own. If you do find yourself in the difficult situation of having to use a strange dumbbell, get some of your dog's saliva on the dowel so he has a chance of claiming it as his own.

The Retrieve: Formal Training

The Problem with the Ear Pinch. When first introduced to the ear pinch I was appalled. I was not about to pinch my dogs' soft friendly ears, and consequently taught them retrieving by even less humane methods. Later I watched members of an Open class pinching away incompetently and developed an even stronger aversion to the method. Still later, I had a pair of dogs thoroughly pretrained for retrieving and did not have an acceptable training method to use for them. A little quiet thought, which seems to help quite often, brought me back to the ear pinch and what is wrong with the ways it is generally used. The basic problem with the ear pinch is that the technique is poorly understood, both by the people who teach it and those who use it. Also the dogs it is used on are not pretrained and are confused. With that combination it is not surprising that the results are unsatisfactory. Properly applied, ear pressure can be a perfectly humane and minimum force method of completing the retrieve training on a dog that has been adequately pretrained.

The Compassionate Ear Pinch. Used properly, ear pressure does not punish the dog and he has control of how much pressure is applied. The dog is placed in a sit. The ear is held as shown in the photo, with the owner's forefinger through the collar ring on the inside of the ear and the thumb behind it, so the ear is held between the thumb and the ring. For clarity in the first photo we show the right hand in pressure position; however, you will need that right hand for the dumbbell so actually the left forefinger goes through the ring and the left thumb holds the ear against the ring. See the second photo. Before someone accuses me of abusing Kitty Hawk's ear, let me reassure you that no pressure was applied to her for this photo session or for the six months preceding it. She always looks wistful. In fact, our difficulty was not her resistance to taking the dumbbell but an excess of eagerness

For ear pressure the thumb is on the back of the ear while the forefinger and collar ring fit inside the ear. (Shown here right-handed for clarity.)

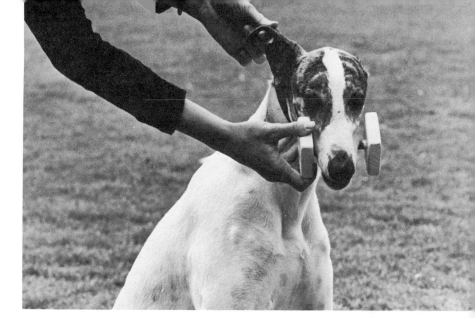

This is a completed "Take" with the ear in the left hand and using a correctly fitting dumbbell.

on her part. The second photo was intended to show her in mid-reach for the dumbbell. In spite of the photographer's being able to stop action on all other fast sequences, in every proof of this shot the dog had already reached the dumbbell and taken it. She was not about to let a loose dumbbell stay within reach while I had her ear in my hand. That is really the secret of the ear pinch. The object is to teach the dog that a dumbbell in the mouth provides unfailing protection from ear pressure—to get the dog to believe that his grabbing a dumbbell will immediately release pressure on his ear. This is why the most important part of ear pressure is not its application but the *timing of its release*. The dog determines when the pressure is released. The exercise should be practiced in an area with no distractions where the owner can pay close attention to the dog and be sure that at the moment the dog opens its mouth the pressure on the ear is released. Uncoordinated owners often pinch away on the ears of dogs that have already taken the dumbbell. Such pinching only teaches the dog that dumbbells make their ears hurt. The pressure itself does not teach the dog anything. It is the release and the timing of the release that reinforce the dog's actions. However, we are getting out of sequence, so back to the basic instruction.

With the dog sitting, collar ring on finger and ear in hand, a small amount of gradually increasing pressure is applied to the ear by pressing the left thumb and forefinger together. The dog's reaction is generally to open his mouth to say, "Ouch." At this point you instantly release the pressure (hang on softly to the ear), slide the dumbbell into his mouth, and cheerfully say, "Take it," or "Fetch." His reaction will be to spit it out so you hold his mouth closed gently with your right hand while telling him what a great dog he is. It is harder for him to spit the dumbbell out if you have his head tilted back. Then take the dumbbell from him. Most of the praise is given while he is holding it, however involuntarily. While being praised he finds it hard to concentrate on getting rid of it. A couple of repetitions of this procedure and the dog learns two things: for some obscure reason you are not going to let him drop the dumbbell, and opening his mouth takes the pressure off his ear.

It is essential that the handler be cheerful in all the retrieve teaching. Often handlers who are not comfortable with ear pressure or who equate it with punishment compound the problem by berating their dogs as if they were indeed being punished. They try to browbeat the dog into taking the dumbbell so they will not have to apply pressure. This is misguided kindness. A dog is much less depressed by an enthusiastic ear pinch than he is by believing that his owner is mad at him. The dog takes his mood from your mood. The owner has to be cheerful. The ear pressure is an impersonal thing that the dog should think he controls. "If you feel pressure on your ear, open your mouth and it will go away." Once he has the mouth-opening response down pat, the dumbbell is not placed in his mouth but is held just in front of his nose so that he has to reach for it. He learns that he has both to open his mouth and reach to relieve the pressure. Gradually he has to reach out farther and down toward the ground.

A sitting dog has trouble seeing an object just at his feet, so by the time the dumbbell is on the ground it should be at least three or four feet in front of the dog. The point at which most dogs have trouble with the retrieve is when the change is made from taking the dumbbell from the hand to taking it from the ground. All this time the hndlr has been working with the dog's ear in his left hand, mostly without applying any pressure, just holding it for insurance and company. At this stage some dogs will look out over the dumbbell without seeing it. Some will lie down on it and look at the handler, which makes for a difficult position to retrieve from. Help the dog. Hand him the dumbbell. A little pressure on the ear opens the mouth to take the dumbbell. The right hand stays under the jaw to keep the mouth closed and tilt the head back, while you praise and call him to you and back up a few steps. Then make a great fuss over him, take the dumbbell, and tell him how great he is. What he is now learning is to go forward on the fetch cue, pick up the dumbbell, turn, and come back to you. Play with him between attempts. Why should he retrieve a dumbbell if you immediately throw it away again?

When he is going out readily and you no longer have to hand him the dumbbell, let him go out all of six feet alone. Gradually the distance is increased. Often at this stage a green dog will run out, touch the dumbbell, and come back without picking it up. Do not be upset. His habits are just incomplete. Send him out again with a "Silly, go get it." If he misses it twice then go out with him cheerfully, hand it to him, and give him extra praise on the way back. We would not want to punish a dog who is new at retrieving for fear of making him hate the exercise. Besides, what a dog needs in any new learning situation is encouragement. Do not do more than four retrieves in one session.

One of the things to watch out for in the ear pressure retrieve is that if you press, even gently, on an ear for an extended period of time, you decrease the blood circulation in the ear and the dog loses feeling in that ear. This is like having no feeling in your foot when you have been sitting on it for a while. If the dog has no feeling in the ear, then ear pressure is not going to work. You have to let him regain blood circulation in that ear before he can even tell you are holding his ear. Generally, when an owner complains that his dog has insensitive ears, it is because he has anesthetized his dog's own ear with steady pressure.

If you are convinced that ear pressure is not the method you want to use, then go back to the pretraining games, which is where ninety percent of the retrieve training is done. With additional playtraining and patience, you may never need to press an ear at all. The better the pretraining is, the less ear pressure you will use. If the pretraining is perfect and the dog is enthusiastic, then no ear pressure will be needed. The goal is to use the minimum force possible.

Ear pressure should not be used on a dog for more than an absolute maximum of three weeks (nine training sessions). If the desired results are not achieved in that time ear pressure is not being used correctly, or it is not appropriate for that particular dog. Two days were sufficient for a willing greyhound with good pretraining. Two weeks were needed for my most reluctant retriever. This training does not produce a finished retriever but a dog through the second stage of retrieving.

All dogs go through three retrieving stages. As puppies and in play they will often free-retrieve most of the time. When they are taught that it is no longer a game, that they have to retrieve every time, most dogs rebel a little. No matter how much they liked it as a game they resist the element of necessity. This is the second retrieving stage. Once the dog accepts the inevitability of the retrieve it becomes a fun game once more in stage three. The trick to retrieve training is to get part two over with as quickly as possible and bring the retrieve back to where it is fun for the dogs. Dogs learning the retrieve make uneven progress. They look good, then have sudden lapses into incompetence, and bounce back, performing well once more. These lapses do not require more training. Quitting for the day seems to help as much as anything.

Ear pressure is not a casual training method. It is one technique in which the application is everything. The trainer has to be extremely alert to release the pressure at just the moment it will help the dog. You will seldom be in closer mental contact with a dog than while trying to determine the exact moment at which to release the pressure so as to encourage the dog's first tentative motions toward retrieving.

It is a good idea to praise the dog after he has the dumbbell in his mouth. If he is praised while reaching for it he will

Whistle, clap, shout, and whoop. Encourage the dog to come back to you fast. This is not the place for any kind of discipline.

often be distracted by the praise and turn around for some more kind words while forgetting to complete the pickup. Once we are past needing the ear pressure and the dog is free-retrieving, the praise which was used during the teaching becomes the only incentive. As soon as the dog has picked up the dumbbell and starts to turn, he gets a whoop of glee and applause from the handler and is encouraged to return at the gallop. If a fast trot is the best he can do for the moment, we settle for that, but the dog is literally greeted with open arms by the handler. In the show ring a handler may have to keep his hands to his sides but that is no reason to be stiff and unresponsive in training. When the dog presents the dumbbell, take it. We'll teach him to hold it for a wait on presentation later. For now, concentrate on reinforcing the retrieve.

A Pinch in Time

It was just another dog show. Having arrived early for once we were going in to locate our ring when I saw the lady and the Afghan Hound. They were just outside the show boundary marker: the lady with a dumbbell in one hand and an expression of very little hope, the Afghan at heel. I stopped my four Greyhounds and waited. Running dogs respond enthusiastically to others of their kind, and a team of Greyhounds romping by would have been more distraction than the Afghan needed during his last practice before the trial.

The lady threw the dumbbell out a few feet and said, "Dog, fetch." The dog remained seated. She repeated the command with increasing threat in her voice. The dog looked sideways, away from her and the dumbbell. She rummaged through his hair and found an ear. "Aha," I thought. "She will pinch him and he will retrieve." But for a moment nothing happened. Ear in hand, she gave him one more futile and hostile command, then waited and finally put pressure on the ear. It was too little and too late, as she led him forward by the ear and pulled his head down to the dumbbell. He picked it up reluctantly, walked back to present it to her with disdain and, on the finish command, did a classic slow motion finish to heel, where he gave his handler a dirty look. It hurt just to watch. I have seen that look before. My instinct was to pounce on the lady and try to help her, but what could I say? Any performance is the result of both the basic quality of the dog-handler relationship and the training methods that have been used. It had taken the pair at least six months to reach their present level of misunderstanding, and it would take at least a month or two of retraining to help the situation. There was nothing that she could be told that would help her through the upcoming half hour. The odds were twenty to one that the dog would fail, and the lady did not need a busybody telling her just before the class why it would fail. At that point the only possible helpful suggestion that could have been made would be for her to concentrate on smiling at the dog in the ring. Imagine that you are heading into the ring with a dog that you are sure will fail and some stranger tells you to smile at it! With the better part of valor we went to the breed ring instead, leaving the Afghan and handler to their own destiny.

For any handler who thinks the situation sounds familiar and who has time to retrain before the next show, here is what I resisted telling the Afghan's handler:

1. If the dog knows how to retrieve, throw the dumbbell at least twelve feet, and better yet twenty-five feet. A pickup from the ground immediately in front of the handler is one of the hardest for a tall dog to make. He is probably looking out over the dumbbell and does not even see it. He does not like to lower his head while that close to a standing, dominant person. If conventionally trained, he knows he is within reach and is most likely worried about the safety of his ears.

2. Give the cue cheerfully, with hope and enthusiasm, even if it is an act. Berating the dog makes him not want to participate.

3. Do not use a reluctant ear pinch. Timing is important. For correct use of ear pressure see the retrieve section. There was no reason to wait for three separate refusals on the dog's part before pinching his ear. This teaches him that he does not have to move until his ear hurts and that he can safely ignore the spoken commands, particularly since they were unfriendly.

4. What happened to the praise? When the dog did retrieve, he got a perfunctory "Good dog" and an authoritarian command to heel. If the dog is having trouble with the retrieve, forget the finish. He can pass without it; but his retrieve should be greeted with glee and congratulations. If the idea is to warm a dog up for the retrieve, I will hand a seated dog the dumbbell just to check to be sure that he still remembers to do a take on cue and to give me a chance to praise him for it.

The Rest of the Retrieve

The rest of the retrieve is the hold for presentation. The retrieve is taught without bothering about the presentation. As long as the dog brings the dumbbell and holds onto it long enough for the owner to reach it, that is great and the dog is praised. We do not want to introduce a delay in the praise until the dog is retrieving willingly. Once the basic retrieve is mastered, most dogs will work faster if the dumbbell is thrown far enough for them to have a chance to run to it. Varying the distance also helps build reliability. Some owners have a very precise throw, placing the dumbbell consistently in the same location. Their dogs are so used to it that if the dumbbell is accidentally thrown farther than usual, they may still run out the usual number of strides, turn where it usually lands, and come back without it. In order to teach the dog actually to look for the dumbbell, it should be thrown different distances and occasionally off-center in a crooked throw. If the dog is used to retrieving after a crooked throw, having one occur in the ring will not be such a disaster. Practice retrieving from three- or four-inch-tall grass, or close to a tree, or from under a bush. The idea is to teach the dog to watch where the dumbbell is thrown and to exert a little effort in locating it. It is not sporting to hide the dumbbell completely. We are not teaching the dog to search and rescue. The dumbbell should be in view, just not as boldly exposed as on a close-mowed lawn.

Once the dog is retrieving well, the hold for presentation is introduced. The presentation is of little use to most dogs. It is a relic from sporting dog training, where the dog is taught to retrieve live birds to the hand, and a bird in the hand is worth two that are dropped at your feet and are likely to fly away. My dogs have yet to bring me anything which, if dropped at my feet, would not just lie there until I could decide what to do with it. However, on to the presentation. As the dog comes back from a happy retrieve, greet his return with a "Sit" cue given when he is still several strides away. Since the dog already knows the front sit from the recall exercise, there is little effort needed to transfer the sit to the retrieve. What many dogs like to do, however, is sit, look up at you, and spit the dumbbell on your foot. For one of these dogs, the sit is quickly followed by a "Hold it" cue. A hand under the dog's chin to tilt his head back and keep his mouth closed will keep him from dropping the dumbbell. Do not pinch his mouth closed on the dumbbell. That hurts his jaws and will make him try to get rid of the dumbbell all the harder. Instead praise him for holding it, then tell him to "Give," and take it from him. As he becomes more steady, greet his presentation with a "Stay" cue; walk a small quick circle around him and then have him give it to you. Or circle around to the heel position and heel him for six feet while he's holding the dumbbell. Then stop and take it from him. These little routines teach the dog that the dumbbell will not be taken from him immediately every time he presents it, so he learns to hold onto it and to wait for the next cue.

Simple bribery is a great help in speeding up of the retrieve. Dogs quickly understand the principle of exchanging a dumbbell for a dog cracker.

Retrieve Over the Not-So-High Jump

Before starting this exercise, the dog should be willing to do a ten-foot retrieve and be familiar with jumping on leash. There is a trade-off in benefits in adding the jump to the retrieve. Dogs that carry the dumbbell loosely (many barely hook their lower canines under it) tend to drop the dumbbell when they first try to jump with it. On the other hand, dogs with no great enthusiasm for retrieving often find the jump exciting, and its use may speed up their retrieve.

The first jump should be knee high to the dog. Do two retrieves on the flat and run over the jump with the dog on leash a few times. Move in close to the jump, no more than a stride back, and toss the dumbbell between the uprights so that it stops a little beyond where the dog will land. This will be the same retrieve that the dog has been doing with a couple of extra "Over" cues. There are two reasons for starting with a very low jump. The dog should be able to see the dumbbell lying on the far side of the jump, and it should be easier for the dog to return over the center of the jump than for him to detour around the side of it. At first he is talked through the parts of the routine. A "Sit, stay" holds him for the dumbbell throw. A "Dog, fetch" gets him up and moving. An "Over" helps him take the jump. It may be followed by another "Fetch" if he needs help at the far side. When he picks up the dumbbell, he gets praise, a "Come," and another "Over" for the return jump. Most dogs will go over and take the dumbbell fairly readily. The beginning dog

Kneeling down will help the dog return to you faster. The dog at this point knows the exercise, what remains is practice to build height.

often has difficulty remembering that he has to jump on the way back also. When a large dog turns back toward the handler, he may no longer be in line with the jump, and it is then just as easy to bypass it. To help the return, back up from the jump while giving verbal encouragement, clapping, and repeating the cues.

Most dogs will come back most quickly to a kneeling handler. Kneeling reduces the handler's dominance and is an invitation to playtime and hugs that few dogs can resist. Once a dog is at the point shown in this photo, he knows all the basic parts of the retrieve over the not-so-high jump. The only difference between this dog and the one shown jumping full height is time and practice. Gradually the talk through is shortened to a single cue as the dog's habits strengthen. Slowly the jump is raised, but no faster than the dog will jump willingly. Jumping a dog well within his skill level builds his confidence. While the emphasis is now on the

Gradual practice to build up to the jump height is all that is needed to bring the dog to full height shown here. Be careful to raise the jump slowly so that the dog retains her confidence. The dog with fully developed habits makes an exercise look easy.

retrieve, the dog should still be run over the jumps and called over them at increasing heights. The jump heights for the retrieve should be lower than those that the dog is free-jumping, so that the retrieve jump always looks easy to the dog. The main work of increasing the jump height is done in the free-jumping. The dog should be sure that he can jump a given height before he is asked to do it while carrying a dumbbell. Do not be deceived by a good jumper's natural ability. Some dogs can jump nearly any reasonable height that they believe they can clear, but they need self-confidence to do it. The bitch shown in the full-height-retrieve-jump photo was pressed to jump too high, too young, and under poor lighting conditions. Not surprisingly, it shook her confidence. For months she would readily clear thirty-four inches but occasionally lost her nerve at thirty-six inches. This impasse was not a discipline problem, and a rest followed by practice at lower levels helped her overcome her bad beginning.

Waiting out Anticipation

Once an eager dog learns the cue for an exercise, he often tends to anticipate the cue and volunteer to start the exercise on his own initiative. Many dogs are disciplined for anticipation, but take a look at it from the dog's point of view. As far as the dog can tell, he is being punished for *doing what he has been taught*, for performing the exercise. That should be enough to discourage him. Do not discipline a dog learning an exercise if he anticipates the cue. Steady him with a hand on his shoulder or his collar until the cue is given. We want dogs that eagerly anticipate the exercises in the literal sense of looking forward to performing them. We also want dogs that wait for the cue to start. The way to achieve both objectives is by teaching the dog the meaning of the word, "Wait." To the dog the word "wait" introduces a time delay between his desire to act and his moving into action. It means that yes, he can do what he intends, in just a moment. This may seem like a rather generalized concept for a dog to understand, but do not underestimate the dog. "Wait" is easy to teach, just by using it in varied situations. The word is always followed by a brief delay, then rather calm praise, and finally by permission for the dog to do whatever the "wait" postponed.

For Anticipated Finishes. The dog sits in front of the handler and before he can anticipate the finish the handler says, "Wait, wait there." The unfamiliar word will usually distract the dog from his intended finish and cause him to look at the handler for further information. This causes a small delay, and he is then told that he is a good dog and gets his ears rubbed. Dogs were not given soft, seductive ears for nothing. This is one situation where the praise is calm and heartfelt instead of normally enthusiastic. We are trying to restrain the dog, and whoops of glee would possibly inspire him to anticipate. If he tries to break under the praise, he can be gently held still by the collar. Then he is told to wait again. The handler releases the dog, and after a brief hesitation cues the finish.

For the Retrieve. Now that we have taken the time to develop our dogs into enthusiastic retrievers, they are going to want to chase the dumbbell as it is thrown, in spite of their being on a sit stay. However, we do not want to discourage their retrieving by punishing them for trying to do it a little too early. For a few months I hooked a finger through Trip's collar to hold her in place as the dumbbell was thrown. After the stay cue and the throw, she was told "Wait," and I would gradually release the collar until she was sitting free for an instant before she heard the fetch cue. This same method can be used for all the exercises in which the dog is required to leave the handler's side but tends to leave a little early.

Steadiness. What the wait cue teaches is steadiness. To the trainer, the dog seems to acquire steadiness very slowly. While the wait seems simple and is easy to teach, it does take time to make it completely reliable. What we are doing is instilling deeply seated habits through patient repetition. The result is a dog that performs because the habits are so strong that it does not occur to him to do anything except respond to the cues. Such a dog is very reassuring to show. I personally prefer it to the dog that has to evaluate for each exercise the chances of safely getting away with not performing correctly.

The Drop on Recall

It may cheer up handlers worried about teaching the retrieve to know that it is not the most difficult Open exercise. The most frequent, poorly executed, and failed Open exercise is the drop on recall. This is especially frustrating since it looks easy and it can be quickly taught the wrong way. The dog already knows the recall from Novice. All he has to do is add the drop. It is most commonly taught by slapping him across the shoulder with a leash end, or catching him on top of the nose with the fingertips in a downward swing, or by "rushing him down"—that is, leaping in and collar-correcting him to the ground. Since the average dog is not going to fight his owner, his reaction when assaulted is to drop. So the dog drops and the owner is happy to think he has at least succeeded in teaching one exercise, especially since he is probably just then in the learning and unrewarding part of the retrieve training. But a strange thing happens. The dog eventually learns the retrieve, decides that it is fun, and gets good at it. The owner starts to show, and the drop on recall starts to deteriorate. The longer the dog is shown, the worse it gets. The dog sits at his end of the ring politely waiting for a second call to come. He walks toward the owner instead of hurrying. He stops and stands, or drops without waiting to hear the down cue. He bows, not going all the way down. He takes thirty feet to drop, sinking lower with each step to crawl to his owner's feet.

Dogs put a lot of imagination into their efforts to make the drop interesting. Why do they do it? There are two basic reasons. First, the drop is a simple, predictable exercise with maximum opportunity for boredom. Second, both the basic nature of the drop and its conventional training methods are punitive. A dog running toward his owner is happy. Watch the Novice dogs' recall. When a dog running in is halted by a down command, he is disappointed that he did not get to reach his owner. He went from the activity of running to immobility, which is not fun. Even worse, most owners yell "Down" on the drop as if it were a mortal threat. Then the slap, tap, and jerk down methods of teaching the drop confirm the dog's suspicion that this exercise is not fun. He is getting both manhandled and yelled at. In this situation it does not take too much intelligence to decide to sit out there a moment and wait for an extra come command. And there is hardly any point in hurrying toward the owner when every step brings the dog closer to that nasty drop.

The Alternative Drop.

The unpleasant methods of teaching the drop are quick and dirty. The constructive way of teaching it is slow. Sorry, but you have to pay for everything. In this case the price is time.

I had a greyhound that recalled at the double suspension gallop. My obedience club folk with their trotting shelties and setters said optimistically, "That is a beautiful recall but you will never be able to teach her the drop." They had a point and I considered it. The drop was not the problem. The conventional methods were available, and they would teach her the drop, but they would also damage our relationship and kill her recall. The problem was finding a way to stay friends through the training and to save her recall. We were having too much fun with it to give it up. In training it always helps to be sure of what you really want from the exercise. In this case I wanted a dog that would drop with the same enthusiasm she showed on the recall. She should think that the drop was part of a game instead of punishment. Achieving this meant inventing games that contained the drop. A little bribery again proved useful. The games are:

Cookie in the Kitchen. This is an easy one. Instead of just handing out crackers at random, first put the dog on sit in the dog corner. "Dog, down." After a few down cues and perhaps some hand pressure on the back of the neck, he reluctantly goes down. The moment his elbows touch the rug a dog cracker slides into his mouth. This is one of the games in which the dog thinks that he controls the owner. The dog is full of energy and wants to bounce up and lick the owner's nose. He learns that he is more or less free to do so but that a lick does not trigger the owner's cracker hand-out response. Only a drop activates that response. Dogs pick this up quickly. Usually a half dozen guided downs that result in food are enough to give them the idea that having their chest on the ground moves your hand to their mouth. This is taught away from the training area. Dogs that are good at it will start to drop whenever you walk past the refrigerator in the hopes of activating the response. Once the dog has learned his part of the game, remember to play it with him occasionally to keep him in practice. He may do a lot of volunteer drops that you do not notice and do not reward with food. He will become discouraged unless you make the effort to reward him from time to time.

"Daaaoouwn!" is not the way the down cue is given in order to get a quick reaction from the dog. Down is a one-syllable word. It is one of the mushier cues since it lacks both the crisp "t" or "p" type of consonant and the sharper vowel sounds such as the "y" or long "e." However, by stressing the "d" and contracting the rest of the word, it is possible to make the down cue into a brisk one-syllable word. Brisk cues produce quicker responses from the dog than do long-drawn-out words. The slower a cue is given, the slower is the resulting performance. This same rule holds true in the signal exercises later on.

The Drop Quick. This optional method works very well for some dogs and owners and not at all for others. It is worth a try for anyone except the less coordinated owners or the owners of shy dogs. It relies on the element of surprise. Most of the taller dogs have the same problem with doghouse doors that basketball players have with house doors. The doorways are too short. As the dog grows, it learns to duck quickly whenever its shoulders touch an overhang. For the dog with lots of clearance at home you can add an obstruction in the run or yard to teach him to duck. Some dogs learn the duck thoroughly just by slinking under the dining room table. Whichever way it is learned, many dogs have an automatic response to start to duck or drop at any sudden impact on the withers (the tops of the shoulder blades). That takes care of the dog's responses. Now for the trainer's.

Try this without the dog. Extend your arms with your elbows slightly bent and place the palm of your right hand against the back of your left hand with your hands slightly crossed. For anyone who has practiced closed heart massage, it is about the same position and very much the same motion. Now, sit down and press the crossed hands very gently against your own thigh above the knee. The action is a very quick pressure as both elbows are straightened slightly and then relaxed. The hands move forward no more than an inch. Because you are using both arms quickly, you apply a lot of pressure for a very short time. Because your hands are already up against your leg, and later the dog, it does not hurt. It is not a blow, and must not become one.

In order to combine the "pop down" with the dog, two things are needed. The dog must be close to your knee so that you can reach him, and he needs to be moving for the pop to have the desired result of causing him to drop. If a dog is standing still with all four legs braced, then quick shoulder pressure will neither surprise nor drop him. He will stiffen up to resist it. So to get him in close, moving, and thinking about something other than the drop, we play with him. At some point in the wrestling match he will come in alongside, or if he is a remote player, a leash can be used to guide him alongside. Both hands drop down across his withers. He is given a clearly enunciated, "Dog, down," followed by a pressure pop. Dogs for which this method works will literally fall away from under your hands. As soon as the dog is on the ground, you are back to playing. A couple of quick scratches on the belly and an "Okay" will bounce him back up into the roughhousing more enthusiastically than ever. We are teaching the drop, not the down stay. He does not have to stay down. If the dog freezes and refuses to drop or starts to shy away from the owner, scrap this method as not suitable for that dog.

The Recall from the Drop

Neither of the above games for the drops have any connection with the recall yet. The drop is taught separately to avoid slowing down the recall. The dog's response in the recall will be carried over into his performance of all the related exercises where the dog approaches the owner. Once a dog's recall has been slowed, that same slowness will be reflected in the retrieves, the signal exercises, and the glove exercise. We try to preserve his speed by not recalling him *into* a drop. Instead we practice drops, and recalls from drops.

The Random Drop and Recall. Once the dog has "Cookie in the Kitchen" mastered, practice dropping him everywhere—in the park, on street corners, out in the yard—and don't forget his bait. Try giving him a "Down" when he is five or six feet away with his side to you (not while he is coming to you). He will likely turn and come. Take him gently back to where he was and repeat the "Down." Give him his cookie and add something new: say "Stay," which he already knows from Novice. If he dropped without help, *you run out to him* to reward him and tell him to stay. You then hurry away from him, turn, and after a moment's hesitation, give an enthusiastic "Come." What we are trying to teach the dog is that immediately after the drop he will have a chance to run to you, which is fun. At least it will be fun if the owner gives the dog enough praise, play, enthusiasm, and goodies to make him think that it is. Leap up and down and whoop a little. Back away from him. Talk to him. Do whatever can be thought of to bring the dog out of the down at a run. This exercise is designed to create a dog that recalls fast out of a drop. It has the added advantage of teaching the dog that the owner will run toward him to praise him. Actually you run to the dog to get there and praise him before he decides to break the down, but he does not know that is the reason for the hurry. He just knows that if he holds his position while you run to him he will be rewarded. It gives him an entirely different attitude about your approach from that of a conventionally trained dog for which a running owner means imminent correction for errors in the group exercises.

Adding the Recall to the Drop. What we have been doing is teaching the dog to drop on cue both close to and at a distance from the handler. When the dog is doing a reliable drop, we try it during a recall. The faster the dog does the recall, the farther out he should be told to drop. If a dog is close to the handler by the time he hears the drop cue, it is too easy for him to come on in and either not drop or drop at the handler's feet. So we give a drop cue with a lot of emphasis and a hand signal for good measure. If the dog looks surprised (after all he has never been asked to drop during a recall before), we set him up for another recall and try again. If he drops, fine. If not we take him back to where he should have dropped and tell him to down and stay. Then we back away from him, praise him, and call him out of the drop. This shows him that he should have gone down and that if he does drop he gets to finish the recall in a few moments. The first time that the dog does drop, *run out to the dog to praise and play with him.* At first release him from the exercise here as part of his reward. Later on, when he is dropping regularly, every time he does so on cue the handler runs to the dog to praise him, and then back off again to do the rest of the recall. If you get lazy and neglect going out to the dogs his performance will deteriorate.

Once the dog knows the drop on recall he will start to anticipate the drop. I then practice three straight recalls for every recall with a drop in it. The dogs quickly learn that the

Open ring means they will have to do a drop, so at practice matches, I will do nothing but straight recalls. If you do not intend to drop the dog at a practice match, it is a good idea to warn the judge. I can still remember not doing so an having the judge signal the drop, and then as I ignored it, signal again and again, bounding up and down at the far end of the ring while I tried to look as if nothing unusual was happening for Tiger's benefit as he did his recall. He is very good at reading expressions. At least the judge's discomfort was worthwhile, as Tiger took his first Open leg the following day. That leads to one more suggestion. At an A.K.C. trial, ring routines are always the same. Practice matches are the place to give the dog ring experience in doing unconventional things, so that the dog is not absolutely certain that it will be just the same old routine when he goes into a ring. Try some of the uncalled-for heeling variations—a cloverleaf pattern or a U-turn to the left, or a step off to the right. The judge may be surprised, but the purpose of practice matches is practice, not qualification.

Group Games

Dogs respond to the group exercises according to their temperaments. A phlegmatic, passive dog is often perfectly happy in the sit and down stays. A dog that lacks initiative will feel safe in the security of an exercise where no action is required of him, and he may do beautiful, steady group exercises. On the other hand, the energetic, outgoing dog will take a dim view of anything that restricts his activity and will regard the groups as a form of punishment. With the passive dog there is not much to teaching the group exercises. He is placed on a sit stay, and replaced on it whenever he moves. Eventually he figures out that the idea is to do nothing, and he and his owner are both happy. That leaves the owner of the active dog still struggling to teach his student that immobility is fun. This problem occasionally leads me to fantasize about owning a perfectly matched brace, one active extrovert for the individual exercises, and one passive pessimist for the groups. But back to reality.

There are two keys to teaching the stays to an active dog. The first is not to overdo the correction. When the dog moves, he should be taken back cheerfully and replaced in the sit with a token collar correction. The idea is to make the dog understand that he is to remain in place, not to make him afraid to move. The other essential is that the dog have something active to look forward to when he is released from the stay. In this way the stay just becomes a long "Wait" interval leading up to a fun game. Sunny did incredibly elaborate stretches after each group exercise. Trip gets to do a few leaps and bite my hair after her stays. Looking forward to that helps her to tolerate these, her least favorite exercises.

From Novice the dog will know how to do a thirty-foot sit stay and down stay with the handler in view. What remains is to increase the duration of the stays and to hide the handler.

If a dog is taught to remain in the position that you have left him and to ignore the other dogs in line, then he has a better chance of holding his position at a trial if the dog next to him should break. For this reason I practice mixed sits and downs where each dog is responsible for holding the cued sit or down.

We spend eighty percent of our time on the sit stay. Once a dog is steady on the sit stay, the down stay is easy. The games for the stay are:

The Freaked-Out Handler. The dog is left on a sit stay. At a distance of thirty feet the handler turns to face the dog and lies down. The dog remains sitting; it's the handler that's lying down. A prone handler is a great temptation to the dog, because a dog will drop on its belly and hold eye contact to invite another dog to play. At this point the dog may come over to see if his handler is still alive and wants to play. If he does break, he is taken back, replaced cheerfully in the sit, and the exercise is repeated. When the dog will tolerate a flat handler as many variations can be added as the handler's dignity will allow.

Stalking the dog on all fours will rivet any dog's attention as he tries to figure out whether his handler shows promise of turning into a "werehound." The objective is to create uncertainty in the dog's mind as to what is about to happen,

The "vanishing handler" teaches the dogs to remain alert on the sit stay. The key is to not leave the dogs sitting bored for five minutes, but for the handler to reappear suddenly every now and then to keep the dogs expecting his return.

or, rather, to create the certainty that some kind of fun is going to happen when he is on a stay, if he just remains awake and watches for it. For some dogs, the most entertaining thing they can think of is food, so we bait them at intervals during the stay.

The Vanishing Handler. To work on the out-of-sight sit stays, once the dogs have figured out the few hiding places that the park offers, we go back to the shopping center where they were socialized as puppies. It has a central promenade fenced by stores, so a dog that breaks is not likely to bolt into traffic. If an experienced dog is available he can be used to set a good example for the trainee. The dogs practice sit stays while the handler goes into a store and does not shop. Instead the handler plays peek-a-boo with the dogs, keeping them in view through the windows. Against the background of merchandise and shoppers, the dogs lose sight of the handler. The degree of distractions available depends on the time picked for the practice. Early mornings are peaceful and good to start with. Holiday weekends will test the steadiness of the most ring-ready dog. Before you try it, the dog's stays should be good enough so that you can be sure that the worst he will do will be to get up. This is not the place to train a dog that may decide to leave entirely.

Jumping Pretraining

Those owners with confirmed fence leapers will find this section amusing, but many dogs need to be taught how to jump. Dogs that have been raised running in broken terrain will know how to jump. Yard-raised dogs may not. I once obtained a kennel-raised Greyhound who actually had to be taught how to run. Faced with a pair of reluctant jumpers I thought about the early training for jumping horses. They are usually started slowly, over short solid obstacles, to develop timing, balance, and confidence, and to teach them to pick their feet up. So I set a plywood sheet four feet wide by twenty inches high across the bottom of one of our gate openings. When the gate is open the dogs can pass through it only by jumping the plywood, while I have to step over it. The pack runs back and forth over it in stride. After jumping it on her own a half dozen times a day for several months, even the least coordinated dog has learned to jump competently. By the way, it is a gate that only I use. The jump would be a hazard to unsuspecting visitors, most of whom are not prepared to run short hurdles.

Once the dog knows how to jump on his own, we can start the training with the obedience jumps. Dogs of some breeds are built for jumping and generally love to do it. This is one exercise where they have a decided advantage over many of the breeds that suffer enough hip and structure problems to make jumping the required height difficult. A dog that is in pain when jumping will start to refuse the jump. Or he will jump half-height hurdles while refusing to attempt full-height ones that place too great a strain on him. This kind of behavior can indicate the presence of a low grade, chronic, or recurrent injury, which is not apparent in the dogs' normal gaits. A good working hound whose enthusiasm fell during her last Open leg was later X-rayed to show an old pastern injury with the beginnings of arthritic complications. Fast-growing puppies of large breeds are subject both to injuries and to osteochondrosis, which can cause recurrent non-specific lameness and joint tenderness. For these reasons I no longer ask dogs under eighteen months of age to jump hurdles at their full competition height. When a dog has superior jumping ability there is a temptation to display it early. This may awe the other owners but adds nothing to the training program. A dog can learn just as much over a half-height fence as he can over a full-height one. For training purposes the obstacle only has to be high enough to insure a jump on the dog's part. For a medium-sized dog, a high jump of from twelve to eighteen inches is a good working range. Similarly, the broad jump starts with the sections crowded close together, and one turned on edge for a two-foot span, which is gradually increased to four feet.

The first time the dog sees the jumps should not be as part of an obedience exercise. The jumps are set up at the beginning heights and widths—short and narrow—and dog and owner jump them together with a cheerful "Over," called just before the takeoff. The dog is on leash to keep him alongside the owner, but it is a loose leash. This is a good place to use the dead ring on the collar to avoid accidentally correcting the dog if he jumps enthusiastically enough to take up all of the leash slack. If there is room, it is fun to set up all three jumps in a row, at minimum heights, and about fifteen feet apart. The idea is to jump the whole series, one right after the other. This arrangement has the advantage of giving the dog something to look forward to beyond the immediate jump and of keeping him moving in a straight line after the jump. Many dogs land off center or cut jump corners because throughout their training they have always been turned or stopped on the far side of a jump. When working with a single jump instead of a series, the dog and handler should keep running for ten to fifteen feet on the far side of a jump before the dog is allowed to turn to the side. It is as important to run out of a jump landing as it is to run into the takeoff. The aim is to produce a dog that runs straight at his jumps and jumps squarely without twisting into an off-balanced landing. In a repetitive activity like obedience, a dog that always lands with a twist to the right is not distributing the landing impact evenly. Many of the heavily campaigned senior obedience dogs eventually develop landing-impact-related leg and back ailments, after years of competition. I have a particular aversion to jumping a dog over any greater than half-height jumps when practicing on a cement floor. No one would ever expect either a horse or a human athlete to display jumping abilities on a cement floor. Dogs have no special immunity to the structural wear caused by repeated landings on an unyielding surface.

Each type of jump presents a different problem to the dog. The high jump is the easiest jump for most dogs. It is simple for the dog to judge the height of the plain white jump. The broad jump is more difficult than the high jump. While a dog has either to climb or jump over the high jump, there is no reason he can see for not stepping on or between the sections of the broad jump. Actually there is no reason other than his owner's and the A.K.C.'s whim. This is why the broad-jump training is started with boards so close together that the dog

The dog and handler run together, and the dog is kept centered to the jump with the leash and an outstretched arm.

cannot step between them. One or two of the sections are laid on edge to give the surface an uneven height and make the dog reluctant to step on it. A section turned on edge will make a dog jump a little higher than he would over a flat layout, and it gives him an increased chance of clearing the jump. Most dogs seem clumsy when first introduced to the broad jump. I suspect this is because it resembles nothing they meet in normal life, and they seem to have difficulty in evaluating its size and shape. The dog in this photo is jumping much higher than she needs to. This kind of jump is typical of an animal jumping blind, that is, jumping an obstacle whose location it is aware of but whose actual size and shape it is not sure of. The dog simply jumps on cue, giving extra clearance. With practice and familiarity the dogs acquire the flat-jumping trajectory needed to clear the broad jump with minimum effort.

The utility bar jump is a most difficult jump for the dog to evaluate accurately. It is marked in flashy black and white stripes, which make it stand out clearly to human eyes. But the dog does not see the way we do. The stripes that make it so visible to us simply break up the bar's outline and camouflage it in a dog's colorblind sight. I have seen experienced Utility dogs jump blindly at the bar when they were looking at it with the sun behind it. The more cautious dogs simply balked, peering at the jump, trying to figure out the bar's height and location. Because the bar jump is visually difficult, I like to include it with the rest of the early jump training so the dog will be as comfortable with it as possible by the time he reaches Utility. When set low the bar is relatively easy for the dog to see against the plain grass or ground. The difficulties show up when the bar is raised higher than the dog's head and he is trying to spot it against a broken background of buildings, fences, awnings, and campers.

The run over the jumps can be used as a reward at the end of a training session or done entirely separately. When the dog is jumping eagerly, the owner can run alongside the jumps instead of over them, holding the leash with an outstretched arm to be sure that the dog is still centered over the jumps. Since setting up the jumps is time-consuming, there is a temptation to get the maximum use out of them and overdo the jumping. The dog should never have to jump more than twelve obstacles at a session. It helps to save his interest for the next jumping practice.

The Broad Jump

All of the exercises prior to the broad jump require that the dog move either toward the handler or away from him. The broad jump is the first exercise in which the dog is required

In the recall over the broad jump the dog learns most of the exercise without having to worry about turning after the jump.

to move at a right angle to the direction in which the handler is facing. The directed jumping in Utility is the only other exercise with a similar crosswise direction. There is no reason to try to teach two new things at the same time (both the new direction and the jump from a sit stay), so the exercise is broken into parts. By now the dog knows how to do the broad jump because dog and owner have been running the jump together. The dog also knows how to do a recall from a sit. The next step is to combine the two and teach the recall over the broad jump. The dog is ready when he is jumping willingly at the trainer's side, either off leash or on a loose leash, without trying to run out around the jump. Set the jump at half the length he has been jumping to make it look

easy. Put the dog on a sit stay several strides back from the jump. Then recall him from the far side of the jump using the "Over" cue in place of the "Come."

The reason for halving the length of the jump is to reduce the chance of the dog's trying to run out to the side. Some insurance against early runouts is to have an obstruction on each side of the jump so that leaping the broad jump is the easiest way through. The local municipal rose garden is a great place to practice it, as the rose bushes on the side of the grass walks do not give a dog much opportunity to run out. In working in the open, a dog that runs out is met by the trainer at the side of the jump, put back on leash, and taken back to running the jump until his grasp of "Over" is firmer.

When the dog is recalling over the jump reliably and enthusiastically (food rewards help), gradually increase the length of the jump. When he is readily jumping three-

In the final form of the broad jump, the handler stands beside the jump. If the dog has the habit of jumping straight, which he learned from the recalls over the jump, then he will continue to jump without cutting the corner even after the handler moves up next to the jump.

quarters of his required show distance, the next step is introduced. Once again the jump is set at half length. Place the dog as if for another recall. Instead of walking on past the right side of the jump to your recall position, stop next to the jump; face the jump, not the dog; point at the jump and say, "Dog, over" with enthusiasm and optimism. If the dog's habits, acquired from the broad-jump recall, are sufficiently strong, he will very likely jump it just as he did for the recall. As he lands, a quick cue of "Come" should turn him back to you and to a sit in front. The trick here is to have him so accustomed to jumping when he hears "Over" that the change in the trainer's location does not distract him.

The keys to the over recall are not to crowd the dog, to

place him far enough from the jump to allow adequate takeoff
room, and to stand far enough back so that he will not have to
land in your lap. Crowding the dog either way can make him
balk or run out. The dog is not to be chastised for stepping on
the jump. He is simply set up to try it again and cued with
more enthusiasm. A fast-moving dog does not have time or
room to step on a jump. Turning a few sections of the jump
on edge will make it look less flat and less inviting to step on.

The Broad-Jump Return

One of the difficulties inherent in a large dog with a long
wheelbase is his large turning radius. This shows in the turn
toward the handler after the jump. The size of the turn often
will bring the dog back to the handler at an angle, resulting in
a crooked sit. It takes a special effort for the dog to remember
to swing his rump around to a straight sit in front. If he sits
crooked, and you slide your right foot forward, it will
encounter the dog. If you tell him to "Front" and run your
foot over his left foot, flank, and haunch, tickling him with
your toes, he will most likely hitch his rump out of the way
and into a straight sit, where he is praised. Eventually he will
straighten up whenever he sees the muscles in your knee flex
and before you can move. Still later he will straighten up
prior to sitting.

Photo by Joan Ludwig

THE SUPERCLASS FOR ALMOST EVERY DOG
The Utility Class Exercises

UTILITY, THE SUPERCLASS

The Utility Myth

It is with a twinge of nostalgic regret that I feel the time has come to expose the myth of the Utility class. The owners of U.D. dogs love to impress other dog owners with highly colorful and embellished accounts of the trials and tribulations that have to be overcome to obtain the title. Anyone with a Utility dog will have some incidents that lend themselves to exaggeration, and, by making the class seem more difficult than it actually is, the owner stands out as a hero figure for having braved the snakepits of Utility and manfully won through to emerge triumphant with the Utility title. It seems a pity to expose my fellow U.D. owners but, shucks folks, Utility is not all that arduous. In fact, some Novice and Open owners are sufficiently impressed by the myth to become discouraged and not even attempt Utility, which is unfortunate. Utility is the most fun of all the obedience classes.

The Real Superclass

Should any reader have reached this point without noticing, Utility is by far my favorite class; Novice, with its repetition, is a bit dull, and Open while more varied is still too predictable. But the mere contemplation of Utility quickens my heartbeat and breathing. Utility is the class where the dog is working on his own volition, where communication between owner and dog is crucial, and where an owner has as good a chance of blowing a performance as the dog does. To a great extent, it is this aspect of having the owner on trial that makes Utility exciting. A large percentage of the nonqualifications in Utility are caused by handler error, often errors that the handler is unaware of. As the handler's self-awareness increases he will begin to recognize the magnitude of the problem. Fully forty percent of my dog's Utility nonqualifications were handler-error caused. The challenge is to minimize the errors.

Understanding Utility

The nature of the exercises requires that the dog make discretionary choices: whether to bring back one scent article or a different one, whether to take the glove in front of him or one off to the side, etc. Each time the dog is faced with a choice, the possibility exists that he will choose the non-qualifying alternative. The fact that the choice may be nonqualifying does not make it wrong; wrongness is the owner's value judgment. If a dog is punished for being *wrong*, this often results in the dog's being unable to make choices for fear of being wrong again. And one thing a good Utility dog must have is the confidence to make choices. Confidence is created by teaching the dog that some choices will receive enthusiastic praise and play while other choices are less desirable because they produce *no* response from the owner.

The number of alternatives available in each Utility class makes passing it a less than even bet. A Utility B class with a majority of U.D. dogs will be having a good day if one third of the dogs qualify. A Utility A class, for nontitled dogs, is having a spectacular day if twenty percent of the dogs qualify. The average show time for earning a U.D. is ten to fifteen trials, but it does not have to take that many for a properly prepared dog. Tiger finished in seven trials, while Sunny took eight.

The Utility High

The life of a dog exhibitor has many kinds of high points. Later championships may seem less important, but no dog owner will forget the moment his first Champion finishes. In lure coursing, there is the fun of finishing a Field Champion or Lure Courser of Merit and the excitement of winning an Invitational Best in Field. There is the rather maternal pleasure of watching your dog's puppies winning in the show ring as the next generation matures to provide one more link in the breed's history. Each of these moments is special in itself, but none of them quite matches the most tension-filled five minutes in all of dog competition—the final long stand of a third Utility leg. The dog and owner are in the ring separated by twenty feet of space and enforced silence. There is nothing to do except think of the months of training extending back to Novice, to think of the traveling and the shows and the persistent fly that even now is trying to settle on your dog's left ear. After the fly moves off to inspect the Open ring and you can breathe steadily again, your thoughts turn to gratitude to the dog who can easily sit down even now and blow it. But he is your partner, and you know that though he might teeter a little to keep your attention, he is willing to hold that stand for twice as long as will be needed for the judge to reach and examine him. What happens then? Well, even experienced handlers have been known to shed a few tears of sheer delight. Suddenly there is a catch in the handler's throat, and the dog's outline becomes a bit blurred to the owner's misty eyes. Then with a shock you realize that the dog is watching you intently, trying to figure out what is the matter and if he should come over and console you. So there you are, caught between instinct toward tears of joy and the necessity of appearing calm and normal to the hawk-eyed dog because the judge still has four more dogs to examine before he reaches yours and it is not all over quite yet. This is the longest five minutes in competition. It is absolutely delightful, and I hope every reader has a chance to experience it at least once.

Hounds and Scent

The hounds that hunt by sight are supposed to have the best vision and poorest sense of smell among dogs. However, all dogs can smell well enough to do scent discrimination. When my old coursing dog went out to play with rabbits, his hunting procedure followed an unvarying order. (Incidentally, for the non-coursing enthusiasts, one eight-year-old greyhound is no match for an adult jackrabbit in heavy cover, but we both enjoyed his playing tag with them.) Anyway, when released, he would first sighthunt for ears and movement. This would be followed by quartering to flush low-lying bunnies. If that also failed then he would track them. He obviously considered tracking to be a last resort, perhaps because it conflicted with his desire to hold his head high and keep an eye on everything, but he could and did track. A nose keen enough to follow aged rabbit tracks is good enough to identify human scent. While people tend to have a self-image molded by Dial soap ads, I fear that the dogs probably consider people one of the stronger-scented animal species. For a demonstration of this theory visit the primate section of any zoo.

All this knowledge didn't prevent me from wondering about the truth of the saying that sighthounds can't work scent discrimination. But at the Santa Barbara K.C. Obedience Trial years ago, the puppies with their shiny new C.D. titles and I watched Utility until a whippet worked scent discrimination. He did not qualify that day but he showed us that we could do Utility. After all, if a Whippet could scent, so could a Greyhound, and we went home with a set of scent articles as a promise for the future. There was, after all, still Open to do first. A year later at the same trial, we showed in Utility. *The first step in teaching any dog anything is for the trainer to decide that it is possible.* Given a thinking trainer and a willing dog, a great deal more is possible than is usually attempted. It is common for the trainer to limit his own attempts instead of going for an ambitious goal and seeing how far the dog and he can progress. Let's not limit ourselves unnecessarily. Most things are attainable if we believe in them.

Scent

Scent discrimination is mysterious because it uses the dog's ability to detect a scent that is below the threshold of our perception. It is easier to understand if we consider using our own scenting abilities to distinguish one gardenia scented article from among eleven rose-scented articles, something that is well within our abilities. The entire perfume industry is founded on man's ability to distinguish large-scale, enhanced odors. Or to put it another way, a blindfolded man in a room with eleven ladies who are chewing garlic and one who is wearing Chanel No. 5 could very likely identify the latter individual and retrieve her. Or, just to give equal time, a woman could easily locate one freshly showered Brut user in a locker room full of post-game soccer players. The mystery in scent discrimination is purely a matter of degree. It may be a mystery to us but it is not to the dog. While this exercise is the one that the handler is usually the most worried about, it is one of the easiest for the dog to learn. It is taught in small steps, however, so the total elapsed training period in months is somewhat lengthy.

Why Do It This Way?

The key to good training is resourcefulness and adaptability, the ability to find a successful approach, to discard methods that do not work, and to keep trying new ones. The methods given so far in this book are not the only ways to teach an exercise. They are just methods for other trainers' consideration that I have had success with. With that disclaimer we can go on to the one exception to the rule— *There is one preferred method of teaching scent discrimination*—and that is through the use of immovable articles.

In one conventional scent-training system the dog is asked to choose between two articles, one that is clean and one with scent. If the dog picks up the scented article he is praised, which is fine, but, if the dog picks up the clean article, he is corrected. That is, the article is tapped out of his mouth. He hears a nasty "No!" and he is made to pick up the other article. From the dog's point of view he has just been corrected for doing as he was told, for retrieving. Dogs do not like being wrong. A few sessions like this will quickly teach him not to go near the articles, because he is punished near them. Then the owner has to double-discipline the dog, first to get him near the articles and then to make him pick one up. This creates problems later on. Watch experienced dogs work. Often, as they give each article a quick sniff, they will linger over the scented article and then leave it and check out the rest of the collection again. That extra long sniff indicates the correct article. It is known as "marking down" an article. Since the dog knows which article is scented, why does he not retrieve it immediately? No, he is not trying to give his owner heart failure. He is trying to decide if he is sure enough of the scent to pick it up and risk punishment if he is wrong.

How can we avoid this training trap? *By making sure that the dog cannot be wrong.* For the initial training the clean articles are immovable. They are fastened down. The *only* article the dog can retrieve is the scented article. Since all he can bring back is the correct article, he is praised every time he attempts the exercise, and quickly learns to enjoy it. At first he may try to pick up every item, but he gradually learns to save time by using his nose to locate the free article.

The Hardware-Store Method of Scent Discrimination

This system requires a lot of miscellaneous equipment but it produces reliable, happy workers. Needed are:

A. Twelve pieces of hardwood doweling
   Large dogs—6″ long by 1″ diameter
   Medium dogs—5″ long by ¾″ diameter
   Small dogs—4″ long by ⅜″ diameter

Doweling comes in thirty-six-inch lengths, which are sawed into short pieces and sanded smooth. Then they are boiled and air-dried to kill the scent of the owner. These clean dowels touch nothing living until practice time. If you think a bitch defending her pups is fierce you should see a trainer defending his clean dowels.

B. One pair of rubber gloves for handling the clean dowels without scenting them.

C. A scent tie down board or tie downs for grass, depending on the stage of training. The easiest beginning scent board is a standard 2′ by 4′ sheet of pegboard. The easiest way of attaching the articles for owners with large- to-

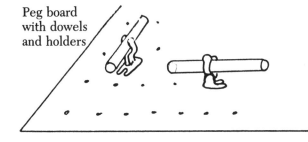

Peg board
with dowels
and holders

Peg board
with scent article
and holder

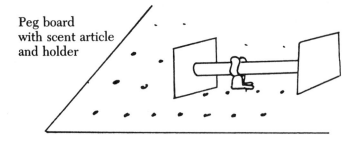

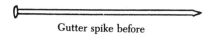

Gutter spike before

Gutter spike after

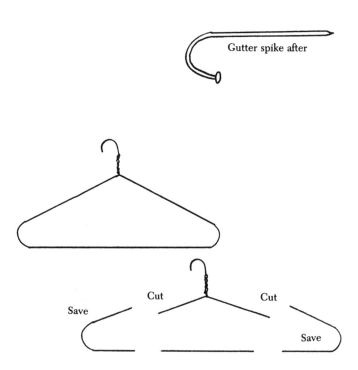

Cut

Cut

Save

Save

medium-size dogs is to use the pegboard fittings that are designed to hold broom handles. The fittings hook easily into the board, and the dowels snap into the fittings. For later practice on grass you will need some clear fishing line, fifteen pound test or stronger, and some hooks that can be anchored in the ground. Some people use gutter spikes, the eight-inch nails that are used to hold roof gutters to a house. They bend the tops over to form a hook. I cut the ends off a lot of wire clothes hangers instead. Each hanger can provide two U-shaped lengths of wire that can be used to hold an article in soft ground.

Scent Discrimination in the Bedroom

This is a perfect exercise to teach in the house, where you will be out of the rain during the winter and close to the air conditioner during the summer. With the gloves on, assemble the scent board, clean dowels, and holders. Clip one clean dowel to the board. Wearing just one rubber glove makes it easy to use that hand exclusively for clean articles and for touching the board itself, while dirty articles, the scented article, and the dog are all managed with the bare hand. Take one article and write an initial on the end of it. If you are training more than one dog, mark one article for each dog. This will be the scented article for that dog for all the initial training. This dowel is kept separate from the others. It is not boiled to kill the scent. It is intentionally just as smelly as possible. Do a little yardwork with it tucked under an arm or into a bra or whatever. Then bring the dog on a leash to where the scent board has been laid out with its lone clean article. Sit the dog and let him watch while you put the scented article on the board in a holder that is clipped to the article but *is not clipped to the board*. The holder is snapped on so that both articles will look the same to the dog. Otherwise he will quickly learn to go to the one without a holder. The holder on the scented article is a dummy. It is never fastened to the board. Take a deep breath and send the dog. He most likely will try to pick up whichever article he reaches first. If he tries for the tied-down article let him struggle in silence. If he then goes to the scented article, great. If, however, he quits working when the first one won't come loose, cheerfully lead him to the other and have him retrieve it. The articles should be about a foot apart. Whether he succeeds at first or needs your help, praise, praise, praise as he brings it back. At this point it is a game for the dog, not a formal exercise. All he has to go on is your enthusiasm. Do not work more than three articles in a row. Frequent, very short training sessions work best for this game. Having a scent board tilted up against a wall makes it easy to play whenever you have a spare moment and the inclination. My dogs were quite happy to try it twice a day, briefly, with a little liver for bribery after each retrieve. If the dog touches an article, that article is discarded as unclean and is replaced with a fresh one before the dog is sent out again. At first the dog will touch the articles often, which is why you need the supply of clean dowels. With practice the number of clean articles on the board is increased slowly to about six. There is always, however, only one scented article. Putting out more than one would confuse the dog. Since he cannot bring them both back at once, he would then have to decide between the two of them.

Teaching scent discrimination is based on gradually increasing the amount of choice a dog has. Developing the complete exercise extends over a four-month period at best. When the dog is working well with six dowels on the scent board, we switch to actual articles. When he is working the articles well, we move outside and off the board. Each article has a six-inch-long leash made of clear plastic fishing line with a loop in each end. The article fits in one loop while either the bent gutterspikes or the hanger ends go through the other loop and into the ground. When first working outside,

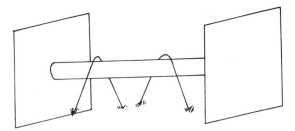

Firm stake down with hanger ends.

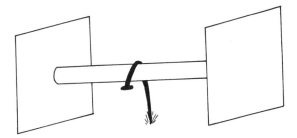

Firm stake down with bent gutter spikes.

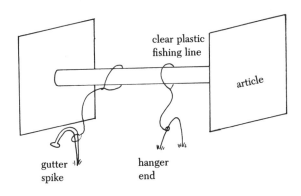

The final staking system
The dog can pick the article up but can't carry it away.

the clean articles are pinned down securely. With time they are given more slack until the dog can pick up one before he finds that he still cannot retrieve clean articles, only the smelly ones. The two worst things that can happen are correcting the dog near the articles and overpracticing.

What flusters the owner most is when the dog manages to get a clean article loose from its anchor and retrieve it. If a dog can get an article loose, greet him as if he were bringing back a scented article. If he can move it then it *is* the correct article for training purposes. After the dog has been praised, make the tie-down system more secure so that it will not happen again. The pegboard holders work fine for the majority of dogs. The minority are those dogs that are really eager, determined retrievers. If you have taken the time to produce one of these, you will likely need a more secure tie-down system. The first time that I sent Trip to the pegboard she braced her feet, tore all the articles out of the clips, and brought all the liberated articles to me in sequence.

Scent Definitions and Hints

Scent is not a mysterious quality. The body constantly sheds small skin and oil particles which the dog is able to detect by smell. When the owner puts scent on an article by holding it, the article bar is coated with skin oils and these particles. This scent can be transmitted just as if the article were covered with visible butter, or chicken fat, or strawberry jam, whatever you prefer to visualize. When a scented object is touched to a clean article or to the grass, some of the particles will be rubbed off and transferred to the new objects. These then carry the owner's scent even though he has never touched them. The dog then may retrieve a supposedly clean article that has been secondarily scented, or he may retrieve a supposedly clean article that was placed on the ground in the same spot where a scented article lay in earlier practice. In both cases the dog is correct. He is

In order to avoid scenting the clean articles, they are placed with tongs or rubber gloves. Later they are placed by another person so that the dog learns to distinguish between general human scent and your particular scent.

identifying the owner's scent with no way of knowing that it is a second-hand scent. Many, many dogs have been failed or disciplined for correctly retrieving articles that were secondarily scented.

A *clean article* is one that has been given good air circulation (aired out) for at least two days and has not been touched recently by the owner or the dog.

Teaching dowels are used at first in place of competition articles, because at first the dog will touch many of the articles. Every article the dog mouths has to be replaced. The hardwood doweling can be boiled briefly and air-dried to remove scent for the next day's practice. A learning dog uses up a lot of clean articles, and competition leather scent articles cannot be boiled.

In scent discrimination things get progressively harder. First the dog learns to choose between articles with no scent and one with your scent. Then he learns to choose between articles with other people's scent and one with your scent. The final step is to teach him to distinguish between your fresh scent and your scent that may be hours or days old. This is done when the dog is performing scent discrimination well by deliberately touching all the articles at the END of each training session. Then for the next practice a few days later, the dog will be selecting from nine articles with old scent and the desired one that you have just touched. Why bother with this last step? You do not want him retrieving at a trial an article that you touched in practice, days before.

Leather scent articles should be stored in a dry place. They mildew in damp surroundings.

Metal scent articles sometimes come with metal slivers still attached from the manufacturing process, so be careful. Dogs can usually find scent on a metal article more easily than on a leather one, which has its own conflicting leather scent. Once they have identified the metal article, however, many dogs are reluctant to retrieve it. Try it yourself and you will understand why. Metal feels uncomfortable against your teeth. It does not taste great either. To compensate, it is a good idea to do plain old-fashioned retrieves with the metal article before introducing it in scent work.

Articles do not have to be dumbell shaped. One successful competitor uses empty miniature fruit juice cans for his metal articles.

Panting and Hot Weather. Dogs scent beautifully in wet conditions and moderate rain. The weather to worry about is heat. A dog that is panting through his mouth is not scenting through his nose. He may wander around a pile of articles for a long time but, until he actually uses his nose, he will be no closer to finding his object than when he started.

Giving the Dog the Scent. The rules allow the handler to hold a hand in front of the dog's nose briefly to give him the scent. Unless the dog is going to be shown by a variety of handlers this move is unnecessary and distracting. By the time a dog reaches Utility, he knows what his owner smells like. From the dog's viewpoint the owner's scent is very strong. Often dogs that have had the hand-to-muzzle cue will sneeze as they start for the articles. The dog is clearing his nose of the hand's overpowering scent, so that he can sort out the milder odors on the articles.

Working the Articles. This is usually interpreted as having the dog move systematically from one article to the next and smelling each one. However, see *Air Scenting.*

Dirty Article. This is not a magazine item. It is an article that has been accidentally scented and that must be removed from the layout, as it will attract the dog. The owner's scent can be applied either by the owner's accidental touch or by contact with a scented article. As we have noted, scent rubs off second hand. The usual dirty article, however, is one that the dog has mouthed, leaving his saliva on it.

Consider this for a moment. Through all the months of Open the dog has been retrieving his own personal dumbbell. How does he know it is his? He identifies the scent of his own saliva on the mouthpiece. The dog has been extensively trained to retrieve objects with that scent. If he finds the familiar smell in a pile of discrimination articles, the article that it comes from is the one he will retrieve. This is why we cannot leave an article on the scent board once he has touched it. It goes in the dirty article pile along with the ones that have accidentally been touched or stepped on. These articles are kept out of the dog's reach.

Air-Scenting. The conventional dog does scent discrimination by working the pile, moving from one article to the next, head down, checking each item for scent. He may inspect every single item several times before making a choice. He looks industrious. The air-scenting dog looks as if he is not even working, and he may be occasionally failed for the appearance of not working. He goes to the pile and stands in the midst of it with his head up. His head may move a little and his nostrils may flare but he looks for all the world as if he is either defying the owner, watching the bitch in the next ring, or going to sleep. After two or three minutes, if the judge has not failed him for apparent inattention, he will suddenly drop his head, sniff three articles, and bring the scented one without ever having checked the other nine. How did he do it? He was air scenting. Scent rises to him as he stands over the articles, and it enables him to determine the approximate location of the desired one. When he knows its general location, he has to make a final check of only a few articles to find the right one.

There are drawbacks to having an air-scenting dog. The most serious one is that in his head-high position he may see something fascinating enough to make him forget about the articles at his feet and out of his field of vision. The second

This dog only looks like he is stargazing. What he is doing is air scenting. Note the article tie downs.

drawback is that a judge may score the dog zero for not working when it is air scenting. The rules require the dog to work continuously. They make no allowance for dogs whose methods of discrimination do not lead them to keep their noses to the articles. The third drawback is that the owner has to read the air-scenting dog very carefully to avoid correcting him for quitting when he is still scenting. A dog corrected for trying to perform quickly learns to not try. A dog standing over the articles and panting is not scenting. A dog holding eye contact with the owner is not scenting. Try to watch a scenting dog obliquely. Direct eye contact, a challenge in dog terms, can freeze a dog in position to contemplate the challenge. As far as the problem of having the dog dismissed goes, it is obviously desirable to have a dog that "works" the articles persistently. However, if a dog's clear preference is to air scent, and he is consistent in locating the appropriate article, I would accept an occasional

Anything that works is worth a try. The only thing that would speed up this dog's scent discrimination was the chance to pounce on her handler at the end of the exercise.

judge's failure rather than refuse to allow the dog to air scent. There is simply no profit in interfering with a dog that is consistently passing any Utility exercise. One of my greyhounds air scents and one works nose to the articles. There is no noticeable difference in their qualification rate on this exercise. *If something works, leave it alone.*

Adapt to the Dog. The nose-to-the-article worker had her own peculiarity. In practice she very reliably would retrieve the first two articles, but if she was sent out a third time she would consistently fail on the third article. It is easy to think that if a little practice is good then more practice must be great. In this case a little practice was good but more was a disaster. The solution was to realize that all she needed for qualification was to bring two articles, and she was doing that. There was no point practicing her with a third article since it only led to failure and hard feelings. So I quit pushing her. She was happy, and our scent discrimination "problem" disappeared. Many training problems are created by the handler, not the dog.

One of my cherished failures was done by the same bitch to another handler. It is easy to appreciate someone else's problems. Sunny had a very clear and simple viewpoint on obedience. If she was corrected, or disciplined the day of a trial, she would wait until she had the wrongdoer safe in the ring and then she would play Sunny games. She has a long memory and an outstanding sense of humor, and had made very clear the consequences of using on her the automatic corrections that most obedience owners are conditioned to. We would not even practice her for the last two days prior to a show to avoid having to correct her for anything. Except for her little oddity she was a consistent worker. At an out-of-town show, both dogs passed the Open B individual exercises. Both dogs were in the same group exercises, and a friend offered to take the extra dog in for the sits and downs. I gave him his choice of dogs, and he chose Sunny, who was doing good group exercises. As he led her to the back of the line she turned toward me for a moment, and he automatically gave her a brisk collar correction. Her expression changed and she went with him. But he knew Sunny well enough to understand what he had done. I asked if he realized that he had just blown the groups, and he agreed. We both waited to see what she would do. The ring was bare concrete, on which no greyhound would voluntarily lie down. As we crossed the ring to leave for the long sit, she lay down, uncomfortable but determined, and did not move until the end of the exercise. He prepared her for the long down. We returned to the ring at the end of the long down to find Sunny inexplicably lying in solitary splendor in the center of the ring. While we were out of sight, she had stood up, walked forward to mid-ring, and lain back down again, a maneuver that I had not seen before and have not seen since. She looked him firmly in the eye as he returned to her. Score two for Sunny. That handler would never make the mistake of correcting her again.

The Signal Exercise

This is a rewarding exercise because it is flashy and impressive to onlookers while still being easy to teach. The hardest part is making up one's own signals. When first trying the exercises I studied books to attempt to figure out the right kinds of signals. Word descriptions of a signal are inadequate, and photos can show only one part of a signal because a signal is an entire hand and arm motion. Consequently, I never could completely reconstruct a signal from books. Actually it would not have helped to pattern my signals after a particular writer's because the A.K.C. allows each handler to make up his own signals. The only restriction is that the signal hand start and finish at the handler's side, and that the signal in between be one continuous motion. Hesitating in mid-signal is known as "holding the signal" and technically is not allowed though often done. The best way to study sample signals is to watch the *handlers*, not the dogs, during the signal part of their Utility routines. You will see every possible type of hand and arm movement. In many cases these will be combined with energetic body English. Some owners look like big league pitchers winding up for a curve ball. They are expending more energy in the exercise than the dog is.

Except for the dogs that hunt with sight and speed, like the Borzoi and Greyhound, most dogs are nearsighted. Perhaps the contortionist signal giver's antics are needed for the nearly blind dogs. What these signals really do is reassure the owners. A dog with good vision can respond to much simpler cues. Sunny would eventually respond just to the smile that I gave her before each signal.

In making up the signals, be sure that none of them conflicts with the signals used to point out the desired jump in directed jumping.

The Signal Order. In competition the signals are always given in the same order. First, the dog is heeled on signal. Second, the dog is cued to do a standing stop at heel. On the "Stay" signal the handler walks to the far end of the ring and turns. He then signals in order, and with pauses in between, the down, the sit, the come, and the finish. So there are six signals: Heel, Stand, Down, Sit, Come, and Finish. In the ring the signals are always given in this order. The dogs learn the order rather quickly and will sometimes go on to the next move before the signal is given. The conventional way of counteracting this anticipation is to give the signals in a different order each time in practice to try to keep the dog from knowing what comes next. It is a method that I would advise against. I tried it and ended up with a willing but confused dog who would guess anyway, only she would guess wrong. It made for a very nervous handler in the signal exercise, and an unnecessarily low percentage of qualifications. Unhappy with that, I taught the next dog the routine in consecutive order, giving him a "wait" cue with a pause and a cookie between each set of cues. With a single exception, he qualified on the signals every time he showed. As long as the class requires them in order, I will teach them in order. Why make things difficult?

Teaching the Signals. With the exception of the stand at heel and the move from the down to the sit, the dog already knows a verbal cue for each hand signal. A great deal of time in obedience is expended in efforts to offset the dog's tendency to anticipate cues. Anticipate is a trainer's dirty word. The anticipating dog is only trying to help by volunteering to do whatever is next as soon as he can figure out what it is. The gentlest way to teach signals is by encouraging the dog to do what he wants anyway, which is to anticipate. At first the routines are run through with the use of both verbal and signal cues given at the same time. They teach the dog the routine order and familiarize him with the strange calisthenics of your chosen signals. Gradually, the verbal cue is delayed a bit so that it comes near the end of the signal. If the dog is getting sufficient praise and rewards to make him want to do the exercise, he will start to move as soon as he recognizes the signal and before he hears the following word. While eventually the "Down," "Sit," and "Come" signals will be given from a distance of thirty feet, they are taught within leash reach. The leash is not used for corrections. It is wiggled to get the dog's attention if he stargazes, and is used a little for guidance.

The Correction for a Blown Signal. The correction for a misread or ignored signal is *not* a physical, collar type of correction. It is the verbal command that follows the signal. By overcorrecting, it is easy to get a dog so apprehensive about signals that he either freezes in place or responds erratically. The secret to the signal exercise is its inevitability. Every time the dog sees a signal, he will perform the exercise. If he does not do so in response to the signal, then he will respond to the following spoken cue. For praise the dog should be rewarded after every single signal, and not at the end of the whole sequence. For the remote signals, this means walking out to the dog for praise and goodies between each signal. It teaches the dog to wait for his rewards before going on to the next response. If the dog is only rewarded for the final step—the come and finish—he will start omitting the unrewarding middle steps and abbreviating the routine to reach the end and the reward sooner.

The Stop on Stand. This is usually taught by signaling the dog with one hand and running the free hand under his flank to hold him in the stand as he stops. What has to be overcome is the dog's well-taught reflect to sit whenever he is heeling and the owner halts. Getting the dog to stand is fairly simple. The difficulty is that the dog tends to walk forward

The Stand Stay: With the standard stay signal, the dog would have to walk into the owner's hand to move, so he stays put.

and stop hip to hip with the owner instead of stopping in heel position with his neck alongside the owner's knee. Some owners respond by following their dog as he slows, hoping to catch up to him. The dog loves this. He will usually keep moving as long as the owner will, and it can take the pair twelve feet to halt.

Faced with a dog that was a confirmed drifter, I struggled along for several months trying to think of an alternative to whopping her alongside the nose for drifting, a conventional method that would cost much more than it was worth in terms of my relationship with the dog. Finally I had the frustrated thought, "Why does she drift in obedience, when she does a perfect stop on stand for breed shows." Sometimes it takes months just to ask the right question. Suddenly all the pieces fell into place. Her show stops were good because I had taught them to her by an entirely different method. The obedience method was not working, although the show method worked fine. This particular obedience method confused the dog, while the show technique was simple and relied on positive reinforcement. Every show dog is taught a free stand for the moment when he is brought to a halt in front of the judge to be looked over. At this point a sloppy stop with feet all awry is a disaster, so we practice good stops. Mine are taught by keeping the car trunk and my pockets supplied with dog goodies. The dog is trotted out on leash and, as he is stopped, a piece of dried or cooked liver is waved in front of his nose. It is just out of his reach, and he is told to stand. His head comes up and his attention rivets on the food offer. It takes a few days to teach and a few weeks or months to perfect the idea that sitting down does not get the goody, nor does climbing up on my shoulders; the only way to activate the owner-liver-feeder mechanism is to stand alertly. As soon as he does stand he is rewarded, so he learns that standing still and posing will get him more liver than reaching for it will. Once he has the stand down, he has additional liver waved under his nose to coax him to make small shifts in his position, to place his front feet evenly and straight beneath him. Then he is baited a little to get him to raise his head and ears and display an alert (hungry and gluttonous) expression. Through all of this he sees a piece of liver between his owner's fingers and his attention is drawn by a quick flick of the wrist, offering and withdrawing the food. The ritual flick of the baiting hand is the basis of a perfectly good hand signal. In fact, it *is* a hand signal, and one that any hand-fed dog is intimately familiar with. Why not use it for the obedience stand? Theories are all very nice, but after the theory is spun, it is time to find out if the dog believes it. So I pocketed some bait and tried it with my drifter. On the third try she did a perfect heel position, head high, stop on stand.

The Down. The down was taught back in Open when we used hand signals for extra emphasis on the drop on recall. Now it is just a matter of practicing to eliminate the verbal part of the cue.

The Down: When first teaching the signals, they can be given with the whole body. Later they are trimmed down to hand and arm motions only.

The first need in signals is that the dog watch for them.

A word and a wiggle of the leash attract the dog's attention.

The Tickle Sit. To move to a sit from the down, a dog has two choices of strategy. Either he stands up and then sits, or else he keeps his rump on the ground and backs up his front feet to lift his body into the sit. This second method is preferred for obedience because his fanny stays in one place. The dog that stands and then sits will often move forward a step or two (or six) while he is standing, which can cost points in the scoring.

To teach a dog to do the walk-up type of sit, place him in the down position and face him. Give the signal and the verbal "Sit" cue. Reach out with your right toe and tickle the ends of his toes, pushing his paw slightly toward him. Most dogs will respond by pulling the paw back. In order to have room to do this the dog has to rise into a sit position. If he leaps up to leave, the handler is using too much pressure.

The Sit: In the walk-up sit, the dog keeps its rump in place and backs up with its front feet into the sit. The handler's right foot is forward because she just tickled the dog's toes to initiate the sit.

The idea is to tickle the tips of his toes, not to stomp on his foot. We tried for a photo of dog and handler toe to toe but were unable to persuade the dog to stay lying down while her toes were tickled. The dog learns to keep an eye on the handler's knee for this exercise, and as soon as that knee flexes the dog will move. For this reason it helps to use a "Sit" hand signal that the dog can see while still keeping one eye on the knee.

The Recall and Finish. These are both exercises that the dog already knows, so like the down they are just practiced with combined hand and spoken signals. The verbal cues are gradually delayed and soon omitted entirely. Dogs have excellent memories for exercises. I entered a local match with a bitch that had been retired for several years just to see how much she would remember. She completed her hand signals one by one until she was sitting in front for the finish. I signaled the finish. She did not move. I shrugged and repeated the signal. She continued to wait expectantly. I thought a moment and vaguely remembered that her old finish signal was a left hand signal, and I had just given her two right hand signals. I tried the same signal with the left hand and she finished happily to the left. It is a great help if the handler remembers what the signals are. The signals must be consistent each time they are given.

General Hints on Signals. Give brisk signals. The slower the signal is, the slower the dog's response will be.

Be consistent. Once you find out which signals work well for your dog, do not vary them.

Be aware of and in control of your habitual hand motions. A signal-trained dog will respond to unintentional signals. Many dogs have nonqualified a class by obeying the owner's thoughtless gesture. A nervous owner can drive a good signal dog up the wall with meaningless gestures. Choose signals carefully. Particularly avoid signals where the very start of the signal resembles the stt of a different signal.

Use bait both to teach the dog to wait for cues and to keep

his attention. The most common signal evasion is for the dog deliberately to avoid looking at the handler. Looking away so he cannot see us is the dog's equivalent of a person's turning down a hearing aid so he cannot hear us. At a trial, if the dog glances away, wait for him to look back at you before giving the next signal.

At eight A.M. on a December trial morning, Sunny dropped onto the frozen ground (for which I was grateful). On cue, she moved back up into the sit. She then turned her head ninety degrees to watch, with apparent fascination, the ring to her left. The judge waited a moment and signaled the recall. I waited for her head to turn back, and waited, and waited. She never looked at me. The judge finally said to call her in. We were up against it. If I called her it was nonqualifying. If I gave her the signal and she did not see it, that was nonqualifying; but at least that way there was a chance she might respond. I signaled the oblivious dog. Having watched me out of the corner of her eye for the entire time, her head turned back to me and she did her recall. She has excellent peripheral vision. Never despair. There is always hope, even when the dog has a peculiar sense of humor.

Subdivided Directed Jumping

All directed jumping is divided into three parts. While it is called one exercise, it is really three distinctly separate exercises, and the parts are rarely combined except in the show ring. The parts are the *go away,* the *remote sit,* and the *directed jump*. On the first cue the dog leaves the owner and crosses the ring in the go away. On the second cue the dog turns and sits in the remote sit. On the third cue and signal the dog returns to the owner by detouring over the indicated jump on either side of the ring. After the finish to heel, the whole procedure is then repeated with the dog sent over the jump on the opposite side of the ring.

Preliminary Considerations

The directed jump is basically a recall with the addition of a detour over a jump. The dog knows the recall from Novice, and it knows the high jump from Open, so all we need to add is the detour and the bar jump. Dogs with good jumping ability love this exercise, so it is fun to teach, but in competition it can be a heartbreaker. Often dogs that are working on U.D. legs have not had sufficient practice with the bar jump. The owner assumes that if the dog can clear the high jump at the required height there should be no trouble with the bar. After all, a jump is a jump right? From the dog's point of view, that is not correct. The dog has been jumping the high jump for months in the Open class. By the time he reaches Utility, he is in the habit of jumping it. For my dogs I

introduce the bar jump early, but most dogs never see a bar jump until Utility. For them the jump is visually difficult to evaluate. Its spindly uprights, striped bar, and the open space beneath the bar make this jump a far less conspicuous target that the solid, white expanse of the high jump. As a result, inexperienced Utility class dogs often run toward the jump on cue and go right past it while seemingly looking for it. This is a particularly painful place for the dog to nonqualify, because it is often the very last of the individual exercises. This very fact contributes to the likelihood of the dog's having trouble with it. Many owners are so elated at reaching the final exercise, while still qualifying, that they proceed to blow it. Don't let up until you are out of the ring.

Play and the Go Away

The go away is one of the more difficult exercises to teach by conventional methods. The dog *wants* to be next to his owner, and the more threatened the dog feels, the more he wants to be close to the owner. Conventionally this tendency of the dog to seek the protection of the owner is overcome by driving the dog away with corrections, or by dragging him away with a line on a pulley. Neither method will produce a dog that leaves the owner happily, like the dog in the photo. This dog is doing what is termed "hauling out." She is in the first stride of a double suspension gallop and is accelerating. She started when she heard the first syllable of the cue, and the handler has not had time to drop her hand through the rest of the signal. In order to get a dog to move like this, he has to be moving toward something that he wants keenly. For the dog that will play, that object is a target toy. It can be a rag or bunny skin. If I am slow in providing a toy, my dogs will retrieve all the litter on the field. The play target go away is the fastest of all the go aways. If, however, the dog is indifferent to toys and rag games but will eat, a perfectly acceptable target is a saucer with a cracker on it. You will not

At the start of the go away, the dog is one stride into the double suspension gallop. Most casual observers believe that the front end just holds a dog up while the arched back and hindquarters provide speed. This photo shows clearly the tremendous pull of the shoulders into the contracted phase of the gallop.

get quite the same speed, depending on just how much the dog likes to eat, but you will still get clean, straight go aways. There are two basic considerations for this exercise. The first is that the longer the go away is, the more speed the dog will use. After the initial learning stages, our practice go aways are normally forty to fifty yards long, as compared to a ring go away of forty *feet*. The second consideration is that the basic purpose of this training is to build such a strong habit in the dog that when he hears the cue "Go" he will have run forty feet before he has time to think about what he is doing. What we want is not a lot of repetition close together; that just bores the dog and makes him slow. What works is limited practice over an extended period of time. We do not do more than three go aways in a session. They are either worked entirely separately from routine training, or else they are the very last thing done after a practice. They are the dog's release. After all, if you did three fifty-yard sprints, you would start to slow down on the fourth one, too. There is no point in working slow go aways, so we stop before they become slow.

Introducing the Go Away. The go away was introduced when you played your first rag games, but here is the formal part of it. Tease the dog with the rag, or give him a cookie sample, depending on what you are going to use for bait. I was once caught between a class trainer who insisted that everyone use gloves for bait and a dog that insisted on food. The resulting compromise was gloves with dog crackers inside. If you use food it should be on or under an object that is more visible to the dog than a small dog cracker. We do not want the dog doing a search routine to locate a cracker in the grass. Do not, incidentally, use a glove. Doing so interferes with the glove exercise. (The bitch trained with the cracker-filled glove acquired, not surprisingly, a tendency to check out all the gloves on the glove exercise to see if any of them contained dessert.)

When the dog is interested in the bait, put him in a sit stay. Walk out twenty feet and put the bait down. Sometimes the dog will break the sit stay, especially if you are teaching this early in the dog's training career, which is when I start it. There is no reason to wait for Utility to start teaching Utility exercises. If he breaks he is not punished, just taken back to his original spot (leave the bait behind) and told to sit and wait. At first, give him whatever your command release word is, for instance, "Okay" along with the "Go." On the first cue he may not move. You push on his shoulder to get him on his feet and race him to the bait with whoops and encouragement. After a few tries he will outrace you to the target and, once he beats you to it, you will never reach the target first again. By the way, he gets the target whether you reach it first and hand it to him or whether he reaches it on his own. He is rewarded every time. He does not have to win to earn it.

This is not a retrieve. If the target is a rag he does not have to bring it back. He should grab it and run with it. For this reason this exercise should be taught in a large, safe area. His reward for doing the go away is the chance to play with the target! This is why the exercise should be something that he wants to do much more often than you give him the chance to do it. Infrequent practice will keep his attention high. Once he has the idea and is doing twenty-foot go aways, the distance is gradually increased to two or three times the length of an obedience ring. This is not difficult. As long as the dog sees the target dropped, he will not be too concerned about its distance. A good rag dog already knows this much of the game. However, in competition we cannot drop a target outside the ring to send the dog to, so now we have to teach the subtle part. We begin to conceal the target so that the dog cannot see it until he has covered the first forty feet of the run. Dogs are built close to the ground. We can see an object on the ground at a much greater distance than they

At the end of the go away the dog gets to kill his target toy.

can because of our greater height. In order to conceal the target from the dog all that is needed, when it is fifty feet away, is to place it in a slight depression in the ground. I use the holes around sprinkler heads in the park. When doing this it is not fair to keep changing your target sprinkler location. Pick one and stick to it. It also helps if you choose one direction and use it consistently. That is, if you normally run the dog from east to west to a target in sprinkler A, do not for the sake of variety suddenly try to send the dog from north to south to sprinkler C. He will probably either stop twenty feet out or turn and head for trusty old sprinkler A anyway. Don't worry about not being able to send the dog in any direction. Right now all we want is to send him reliably in one direction. I practice go aways in two different park areas. In each one we have a standard go away direction, and on that line there are two target sprinklers. Both are on the same go away line, one is just farther out than the other. If the dog sees that the first sprinkler does not have the target, he knows that if he keeps going on the same line the second sprinkler will have it. It is interesting to see just how much faith a dog can have.

We once had a judge from out of state set the scent articles in the center of the rng between the jumps. This used to be a common location but is seldom seen now. My dog and I had never seen it. It requires sending the dog out in the same direction as if he were doing a go away. Tiger went out to the articles, through the articles, past the articles, and continued under the far ring rope, just as he had been taught, on a very nice go away. There was a vacant athletic field beyond the ring. It was a miserably hot day. He had just taken the points in breed and I was feeling rather mellow. Curious to see just how far he would go, I didn't interfere. He was trotting along fifty yards out when the judge suggested that perhaps I had better call him or we might never see him again. He would just disappear into the west, like the hero at the finish of a western movie. I called. He returned along the same line and picked out the correct scent article on his way back. Oh well, he always did like the go away better than scent discrimination. Tiger is not generally noted for his sense of humor. That distinction goes to his sister, Sunny, but every dog has his day and this was Tiger's. On the long stand, he sat. On the long sit he lay down. And on the long down, which he always passed (except for this day), he stood up. That was the last time we entered obedience in temperatures in excess of 100° F. He had made his point. Actually our first plus 100° F. trial should have been enough. He retrieved the correct scent article and with eloquent expression and great feeling spat it out on my foot. Some owners are a little slower to train than others. It took two tries for him to teach me that we would both rather spend cool summer days in Santa Barbara than suffer through the heat of the inland deserts. When a sport is not fun, why persist? Persistence in the face of adversity is a fine old American tradition, but there is not much to admire in needless and pointless discomfort.

The next step in the go away is to progressively conceal the target. At first it is on the ground next to the depression. One run at a time, it gradually sneaks farther and farther into the depression until, after a few weeks, it is entirely out of sight from the dog's starting position. The important part is that the dog has faith that it is indeed there, whether he can see it from the start or not. We are slowly strengthening his habits. Do not send him out unless the target is there. Do not break the faith at this point. If he overruns the target or has trouble finding it, run out and show him where it is, don't let him start to circle and hunt. In the beginning we let the dog watch us hide the day's first target. Later on, as he develops reliability, we hide the first target before the dog is brought out on the field. Eventually he comes to believe that when we tell him so, there will be a concealed target in position, even when he has not seen us go near the place.

Do not be concerned that the dog is always being sent to a specific location. Later we will transfer this orientation to the Utility ring, where he goes down the center of the ring between the high and bar jumps. As long as the dog is used to going *straight* for fifty yards he will go straight between those jumps to the far ring rope. We simply start setting the target along the line that we want him to take, and the dog starts to use our direction and the jump location to orient himself in the ring. The target is occasionally set outside the ring to teach him not to stop prematurely at the ring ropes. Even when the dog is doing ring go aways, most practice go aways are still done in the open with the sprinkler heads and the long go away. If we neglect this, the dog will lose speed and distance in the exercise.

The Remote Sit for Food or Play

In the ring, after the dog has done his go away, he is supposed to turn around and sit facing the handler to await the cue to jump. It does not always work that way. On a warm afternoon at the Santa Barbara Kennel Club Show, I watched a heavily coated dog do a nice go away only to ignore the "Sit" cue. He ducked under the ring rope and went directly to his owner's canopy where he lay down gratefully in the shade and refused to move. In theory, though, the dog is supposed to sit inside the ring rope. Back in the Open class the dog was taught the remote down by guiding him into a down and throwing him a cracker for each down until he would drop any place within forty feet of the handler. We can also use bait to teach the remote sit. The handler has to wait out the initial confusion period when the dog remembers the down training and does volunteer drops instead of the requested sits. You just keep picking the dog up before giving him the food. The dog will probably wish that the owner would make up his mind but will eventually realize that you do not want drops any more.

In the second stage of the go away the dog is told to turn and sit.

When she does sit, she is rewarded by having the toy thrown to her.

To avoid the confusion, it is nice to teach a play sit. First I romp with and tease the dog with the fur piece. Then I suddenly conceal it behind me and give the sit cue. Should the dog sit, it hears a quick "Stay" and I back away until there are fifteen feet between us. The distance reinforces the stay and builds the dog's anticipation when the fur is brought back into view. A few more "Stays" may be needed at that point to keep the dog where he is. He is waiting for the next move. The fur is thrown to the dog and he gets to take off and play. What the dog is being taught is that whenever he heards the words, "Dog, sit," if he sits quickly and looks expectant he will be on the receiving end of a fuzzy toy. This is one of those exercises where the dogs think that they are training us, teaching us to throw them bunny skins. Old white athletic socks are an acceptable substitute for Korean rabbit skins, and are more likely to be found in the average home.

The dog may not sit on the first cue. He may stand, or drop, or recall instead. The correction is to put the dog gently in a sit stay, which he already knows, and to back off to establish the fifteen-foot separation distance. This teaches the dog to respect the distance, and that he won't be thrown his toy until there is at least that much distance between dog and handler.

The Comic-Strip Method of Directed Jumping

Given enough pictures of this exercise we could omit the written explanation entirely. The directed jump is a crooked recall done over a jump. In order to achieve it, we start with a straight recall. The next step is to do straight recalls over the bar jump. The handler is kneeling in the first photo to give the dog confidence and to increase his speed. Kneeling reduces the handler's dominance and is an invitation to play, in the dog's body language. The bar jump is used as the teaching jump in order to give the dog the maximum possible practice with it. The teaching could be done just as well with the high jump, but after the dog knew the directed jumping, we would still have to familiarize him with the bar. To save that effort, I do all my early directed jumping with the bar jump. It is also lighter and easier to carry than the high jump.

At first the bar is set very low. It should be barely high enough to require the dog to jump. For a twenty-six-inch-tall dog, an initial six-inch jump is fine. The jump is low enough to make the recall fun. The dog shown in photos 66 through 68 is using an intermediate height jump. Her intense facial expressions are the result of her concentration. She is still trying to learn to evaluate the bar's position properly.

The first step in the directed jumping is a straight recall over the bar jump. This dog started to practice at half this height. The handler is kneeling and reaching out to the dog to encourage it.

With the dog square with the jump, the handler moves off center. As the signal is given the handler takes one step toward the center of the jump so that the dog-to-handler eye contact is over the jump.

When the dog is doing confident recalls over the jump, we gradually add the detour. There are four steps. For all of them the dog is twenty feet back from the jump on one side while the handler is twenty feet from the jump on the opposite side. What changes are their relative positions sideways. First, in the straight recall, the dog, jump, and handler are all lined up. Second, the dog and jump are in line but the handler is off to one side. Third, the handler and the jump are in line but the dog is positioned off center. Finally the dog and handler face each other with the jump ten feet off to the side. This exercise is saved from being as dull as its explanation sounds by the dog's jumping ability and enthusiasm. But then the dog does not have to read the explanation.

The dog is placed on a sit stay squarely in front of the jump but the handler starts to edge to the left, moving a little farther with each practice sesion. For each jump, start with your feet together and hands at your side. As you give the "Dog, over" cue, take one large step toward the center line of the jump and hold the signal. What a beginning dog concentrates on are the owner's face and hands. The dog does not care where your feet are. If he can see your face and hand framed between the jump uprights, he is going to jump, instead of coming straight to you and bypassing the jump.

Problems

If he does run around the jump, it means one of four things (take your pick). The most common two are either that the jump has been raised too fast or that the handler has moved too far off center too quickly. In those cases you lower the bar or move back toward the center line and proceed more slowly. The third possibility is bad footing for the takeoff. The cause can be bare concrete or wet grass, both of which are slippery. The dog will have more confidence if the jumps are set at half their normal height. The last possibility is low-grade lameness. A lameness of such a mild form that it is not seen in the dog's gait can be revealed by a reluctance to jump. One of the most common causes for the early retirement of sporting and working dogs from obedience is the discovery of hip dysplasia when the dog is X-rayed to see why he is having trouble clearing the jumps. The sight-hounds seem to have difficulty with arthritis settling into old injury locations. The speed of their play and their slender construction understandably make the running hounds a bit more accident prone than the average dog.

Both Sides

Once the dog will take the jump with the handler five feet off center, we repeat the procedure for the other side of the jump. If the handler first moved off to the left, now he works his way out to the right. Do not be impatient with the dog if he seems slow in realizing that you simply want him to reverse the exercise. Knowing an exercise in one direction is not enough. It has to be taught in both directions. It is like ice-skating, where knowing a certain turn to the right does not help at all if you want to try the corresponding turn to the left. Each direction has to be learned and practiced separately.

The end result is a dog that will respond to either right or left hand signals and will jump even though the handler is off to one side or the other. At this stage, the dog is still centered in front of the jump. Once that is learned, we go on to the third step. Here the jump and handler are lined up, but each time the dog is heeled into his starting position, that position is farther off to the side. He will still be twenty feet away from the jump to give him takeoff space, but he will be placed so that he has to detour to the jump deliberately. This is fairly easy for the dog that has had to retrieve a lot of crookedly thrown dumbbells. Whether the owner was practicing off-center throws as we recommend or whether he just has naturally poor aim, the dog that is used to coming back over the jump from a lot of strange locations already knows how to detour to a jump.

Runouts and Unders

The best solution to runouts is not to press the dog too hard. Dogs will run out when they are worried about their position, or the jump height, or are getting sore or tired. However, even a good dog may occasionally be confused and miss the jump. You can usually read this in the dog's approach while he is still ten feet on the far side of the jump. The correction is for you to run forward and meet him next to the jump. You then take his collar, lead him back to his side, and lead him over the jump. This is what was happening in the previous photo, except that the dog was distracted at the

If the dog bypasses the jump, it is met beside the jump and guided over. Used to setting her own stride, this dog got flustered and knocked the bar off. The bar is set with an upright facing each way so that one end of the bar will fall no matter which side it is hit from. This gives the dog clearance, and she will be praised on landing just as if she had not needed help.

change in routine and hit the jump. This dog is not used to being hand jumped. The correction is done happily and is not punishment. The dog is praised on the far side just as if he had jumped on his own.

A quick word about setting up the jump: If the dog is jumping from the same side each time, then the bar goes on the side of the uprights away from the dog's approach. This is so that he can knock the bar off its balance pins without having also to knock down the uprights. When the owner is working a dog back and forth over the jump, one upright is placed on each side of the bar so that at least one end of the bar will drop, no matter which side it is hit from. Even when only one end of the bar falls, it will give the dog space to clear the middle. If a dog regularly hits a jump, lower it. Time and experience will give a dog the confidence to clear the required height. Pressing for too much height early can make the dog jump-shy and teach him to run out around the edge of the jump. To the dog, the jump should always look easy.

In the final step everybody lines up with the jump again, and this time *both* the dog and owner gradually move to the side. The end result is for dog and owner to face each other with the jump off to the side and the dog detouring over it on his way to the owner. After one side is secure, we practice in the other direction to keep the dog from acquiring a preference for either the right or left hand jump.

Worst Possibles

It is a great help to practice worst possibles. For Open this means practicing retrieves after unfortunate dumbbell throws. For directed jumping it means practicing jumping from the position the dog would be in after a very poor go away. These photos show this sequence. First the dog is heeled out and placed in a sit position in the worst position she could assume in the ring. This is where she would be had she done a crooked off-center go away to the ring corner farthest from the jump she is supposed to take, and then sat with her back to the jump. It is a position quite commonly seen at a Trial. It is usually the result of the dog's having previously retrieved a glove from that corner in the directed retrieve. If a dog sits with her back to a jump, some judges out of pity will call for the jump that the dog is facing. Others delight in requiring the jump that is the farthest away. To be ready for these, my dogs spent so much practice on crooked positioning that, if I set them up in front of one jump with

The go away is not used to place dogs for routine directed jumping practice. The dog is heeled out and placed in the desired location. Here, it is being set up to practice jumping from poor ring locations. When the dog is ready to show, then the go away, the remote sit, and the directed jump are combined in the practice run throughs, but only for the first two jumps of the day. To practice additional jumping, we go back to placing the dog in position.

their back to the other one, they wouldn't even look at the jump in front of them. They knew that they were going to have to turn around, run across the ring, and clear the far jump. It is easily taught. You just keep moving the dog across the ring the same way that he was moved out of line with the jump, gradually. By the time the training is finished, you should be able to send the dog over either jump from any position along the back ring rope.

This was especially useful with Sunny. I taught her the go away before finding the proper way to do it. We went through three methods, and the result was so much mistraining that she ended up with intermittent crooked go aways that kept turning up at inconvenient times. We would be at a trial and she would end up in the far ring corner with her back to a jump. The judge would sympathize with us and mentally write her off as failed. I loved the judge's surprise when she would race the full width of the ring to take the indicated jump.

By building up the distance gradually, we can create a dog that will jump from any location.

This is still a practice type cue. The hand signal is being held and the handler has stepped toward the jump. In competition the allowed cue is a verbal "Dog, Over," and a single arm motion.

The Signal

Before you actually show in Utility, the signal is gradually made briefer and the step toward the jump omitted until the dog takes direction from a single wave of the arm and a verbal "Dog, over" cue.

An Object Lesson

In my first trial for Utility, both Tiger and Sunny were entered, although I really had little hope for Tiger's readiness. Sunny was about a month ahead of him in her training at that time, but as long as we were making the trip it seemed pointless not to enter them both. (Besides, I did not want to admit to Tiger that I did not think he was ready yet.) Sunny added an extra drop to the first exercise (Signals) and nonqualified. That took the pressure off. I traded her for Tiger and went back into the ring with no particular hopes. I was watching Tiger's back as he went out in the go away when I realized that he was working smoothly and passing very nicely. I almost stopped breathing. Go aways were his specialty. He pivoted to face me and sat precisely centered with his shoulders against the ring rope. The judge said, "The high jump on your right." I have always had difficulty telling right from left in moments of stress so I took a quick glance to my right to be sure that the jump there really was the high jump. Most of my dogs learn to recognize this slight turn of the head as I check to be sure that I'll be sending them to the correct jump, and they prepare to head for the jump that I've looked to. Tiger took the high jump with enthusiasm and did his final go away.

He sat waiting for the signal to send him to the bar jump, and I grew overconfident. Pride still goes before a fall. He was working like an experienced dog and making the whole class look easy on a day when the U.D. dogs were having a miserable time qualifying. My class trainer was outside the ring just behind me, and he cared if his students passed. The crowd was packed to see the greyhound's first try at Utility. And I blew it. There are several aids that can be given in the cue for the directed jump. Things like my normal glance to the left to be sure that the bar jump is really on that side, a move that might also draw the dog's attention to that jump. The cue does not have to be a flat "Over." It can be "Tiger— Over." The dog will be on his feet at his name, taking his direction from the arm signal. This delays the "Over" a bit, to where it can reinforce his inclination to jump as he is headed toward the jump, or at least looking at it. I ran through the available aids that I could give Tiger, and, because he was working well, and to *show off* I gave him a flat "Over," and the hand signal, with none of the aids that he was used to in training. Taken by surprise by the change in my cue, he ran for the bar jump but was off to one side and stopped perplexed, on the outside of the upright, looking for a bar to jump. He had been carrying a 196 score. Do not let pride make you refuse to help your dog, particularly if the dog is inexperienced in the class. It is not worth it. Having him qualify with a second place the following weekend emphasized the fact that I was the one who had failed him the first time. I had allowed the opinions of the spectators to divert me from what I should have been concentrating on—Tiger and our communication. *When in the ring, the dog is the only one that matters.* Do not change your cues in the ring.

The Directed Retrieve

The heart of the directed retrieve is the ability of the dog to do a good pivot at heel. When the gloves are set out by the ring clerk, they are positioned behind the dog and handler. In theory this is done to keep the dog from watching them laid out, but, since all the dog has to do is look back over his shoulder, some dogs peek. The judge indicates a particular glove by number, and the first thing the handler has to do is remember which glove goes with which number. It is easy to

The directed retrieve sequence: The gloves are placed on the ground behind the dog and handler.

tell which glove is which when you are facing them because they are in sequence one-two-three from left to right, with the left hand glove numbered one. The tricky part is that when the judge tells you the number, your back is to the gloves. More than one handler has ended up facing the wrong glove. However, once the handler figures out which glove he is supposed to turn to, he does a pivot in place and hopefully the dog turns with him. This is where the quality of the pivot shows up. If the dog has been taught to go *straight* out and to retrieve whatever is in front of him, he will do just that. If dog and owner are both facing glove No. 1, the dog will retrieve glove No. 1. If the pivot was sloppy so that the handler is facing No. 1 but the dog is sitting crooked facing glove No. 2, then the dog will go straight out and retrieve glove No. 2. Therefore we emphasize good pivots that end in straight sits. We get them by practicing pivots and by calling on the dog to straighten up if he needs to. This is done without bothering with the retrieve. Since dog and handler

On a "Heel" cue the dog and handler pivot to face the desired glove. This is where perfect pivots pay off.

If, at the end of the pivot, the dog and handler are both facing the same glove there is hope of passing the rest of the exercise. At this point the dog has generally made up his mind to retrieve whichever glove he has in view.

On the hand signal and verbal "Fetch" cue the dog goes straight out to the glove.

As the dog is making the pick up, the handler should no longer have her hands behind her back. For all the exercises where the dog comes toward the handler, the handler's arms are supposed to be down at her sides.

The dog brings the glove back without playing with it, dropping it or mouthing it. Actually dogs often do all three things to the glove. They like to inject a little fun into this exercise. Having presented the glove, the dog waits expectantly to be praised and/or fed.

Sometimes the dog does not come straight back with the glove. It is always fun to show a dog that has a sense of humor. This is Sunny, belly up.

are not going anywhere in a pivot it is possible to practice quite a few pivots in less than two minutes. It also does not take any space, and is the ideal exercise when you have neither time, space, nor equipment to practice anything else. *Perfect pivots pay off.*

Sunny would eventually straighten her sit for a quizzical look and a lifted eyebrow. She also had the endearing habit of picking a glove to stare at. If she was sent out she would retrieve the glove her nose was pointing at. If she was not sent out promptly, then she would pick another glove to stare at and would retrieve that one if sent. She just cycled through the gloves until told to retrieve and would bring whatever she was looking at when she heard the cue. It was reassuring.

All dogs are different, so Tiger had his own system. He performed clean pivots and had the desirable high percentage of straight sits, which was fortunate because once he had his rump on the ground and his attention on a glove, there was no chance whatever of distracting him to a different one. He had to get it right the first time because he would sit endlessly targeted on the wrong glove.

Why has there been no mention of hand signals so far? The hand signal is redundant and of no benefit. As long as the handler is allowed to face the desired glove, the dog is perfectly capable of taking his direction from that of the handler. All that is needed is a good pivot and a straight go away. An additional hand signal can distract the dog. He turns his head to watch the owner's hand and starts out without concentrating on a particular glove. Once he is moving, he will retrieve whichever glove he sees first, and the owner can only hope it is the correct one. For the judges that insist on a signal, I do practice signals *after* the dog is steady on the directed retrieve and is therefore not distracted by the signal. The signal would really be of use only if the handler had to stand in a fixed position and send the dog in a variety of directions. That way the dog would not be able to take direction from the handler's position.

The pivot was taught first in advanced Novice, but for those who hoped they would never need it, here is the explanation again.

The Pivot. Starting out at heel, the dog is given the heel cue and the handler pivots an eighth of a turn to the right. The dog is called, guided with the leash, and told to "Sit straight" to get him into the new heel position. When he has mastered the pivot to the right, the left pivot is introduced. This is more difficult for the dog. Put tension in the leash so he cannot move forward. Give the heel cue and turn toward the dog. Nudge him in the shoulder with your left knee to start him backing around. If his rump swings out from the heel position instead of toward it, guide his hip with your left hand. The first turns to the left should be very small. If he moves and sits crooked at first, praise him and then take a step forward and tell him to sit straight. Eventually he will be able to back into a straight sit, but that is asking too much of a dog that is just learning to pivot. The pivots in both directions teach the dog to adjust his position to stay at heel.

THE INNER WINNER IN THE RING
How To Be a Winner No Matter What Happens

Ring Wisdom

Many strange and wondrous things happen when a handler decides that his dog is ready to be shown. There is a fey and unreal quality to some performances at an obedience trial. It is as if the two hundred feet of ring rope creates a magic circle within which anything is possible. How can a well-trained dog and a hopeful owner achieve a state of total disaster so quickly? Basically because the owner's time and effort have been spent in learning about dogs and dog training. Meanwhile he has not been studying what happens in the ring. Show techniques and ring procedures are a separate area of learning seldom taught in obedience classes. They often are not even mentioned. I was introduced to them at my first obedience trial. Totally inexperienced, I arrived at the ring to

The Inner Winner In The Ring—How to Be a Winner No Matter What Happens.— ". . . It is also essential that the dog demonstrate willingness and enjoyment of its work, and that smoothness and naturalness on the part of the handler be given precedence over a performance based on military precision and peremptory commands." A.K.C. Obedience Regulations—Page 2, PURPOSE.

encounter a kindly Novice A judge. He asked if we had shown before.

"No."

"But you have been to practice matches," he asked hopefully.

"No."

Still optimistic, he persevered. "But you have been to your class graduation?"

"Not yet."

The judge looked a bit wistful and cheerfully invited us into the ring. It occurred to me that there was still more to learn. . . .

Pass or Fail?

Exhibitors are often harsher judges of their own performances than the licensed judge is. Most trial judges want to see the exhibitor qualify, and they know considerably more about the rules than the beginning exhibitor. The exhibitor may think that any errors in performance on the dog's part will mean failure. The judge knows that only certain errors require a nonqualifying score. The majority of errors are "points off" errors for which a minor or substantial deduction will be made from the score, but the dog may still qualify. It is fun at a trial to be able to tell a suffering owner that the failure he has just described is only points off and that he is probably still passing. When trying for her first C.D. leg, Sunny sat up in the last seconds of the long down as the handlers were returning to their dogs. My Novice heart fell, but some instinct (at that point it certainly was not knowledge) told me to wait until the scores were handed out. It was a very hot show and a long wait, but worth it to find out she had qualified minus a few points for her premature sit. When in doubt, wait for the final scores to be handed out. The A.K.C.'s *Guidelines for Judges* recommends that a judge tell the exhibitor when a dog does not pass an exercise, and most judges do. As long as the judge has not told you that a specific exercise was failed, there is still hope. There is also an area covered by the judge's discretion, where he may choose to rejudge a dog on a specific exercise if it was interefered with because of unusual circumstances. This can be anything from being run over by an Old English Sheepdog to being screamed at by an irate bitch.

The Good Book

A surprising number of exhibitors show little familiarity with the obedience regulations, though they are not hard to obtain. The American Kennel Club is happy to send a free copy to anyone who requests it. The regulations are updated in January of each year. However, they may be a bit stupefying to read the first few times. Hot and heavy arguments take place each year over the meaning of individual sentences. Obedience regulations are as subject to interpretation as breed standards.

The easiest way to get the regulations under control is to color-code a copy. I underline the principal features of each exercise in green. These are always found in the first paragraph of the exercise description. The section on scoring the exercise gets coded red for the things that require a zero score or more than half of the points off, yellow for substantial deduction faults, and blue for minor faults. This way it is possible to get the major, minor, and disastrous types of infractions sorted out.

Do not neglect Chapter 2 just because it does not describe specific exercises. Its regulations apply to the overall performance and to judging. It is also useful to request a copy of the *Guidelines for Judges* from the A.K.C.

Beware of Second-Hand Rules

There is no substitute for studying the rules yourself. At any obedience trial or dog training class there is no shortage of well-intentioned people who are eager to tell you what the rules are, but a strange thing happens when rules are passed on by word of mouth—the same thing that happens in the old party game where a dozen people relay a message through a human chain. When the first person reveals what the initial message was, and the last one tells the message as he received it, the two versions rarely resemble each other at all. The written A.K.C. rules and regulations are the only true authority. The following statements are samples of things I have been told are part of the rules:

You cannot heel a dog with your hands in your pockets.
If a dog does an automatic finish, it is failed.
You cannot dampen a dog down on a hot day.
You can't show a dog in a leather collar.
If a dog drops a dumbbell and picks it up again, it will fail.

All of the above statements are wrong. Beware of second-hand advice, no matter how well intentioned it is. *Take a copy of the regulations along to the trials.*

THERE IS A FIRST TIME FOR EVERYONE

How to Enter a Dog Show or Obedience Trial

Dog shows and obedience trials are generally held simultaneously on the same show grounds. Occasionally a dog show will be held without its accompanying obedience trial, and some of the largest obedience trials are held independently by obedience clubs. These trials are large because they generally offer more than the five basic classes of Novice A, Novice B, Open A, Open B, and Utility. A large Obedience Trial will have Utility divided into Utility A and Utility B. In addition it will have special classes for Novice Y, Graduate Novice, Veteran, Brace, Team, and Versatility. The results of the special classes are not reported in the *A.K.C. Gazette* and do not count toward any obedience titles. They are just for fun. All of the special classes except versatility are variations on the Novice class.

Novice y is Novice except that all the work is done with the dog on lead. It is for the dog that is not yet ready for Novice off-lead work.

Graduate Novice is for dogs that have their C.D. titles but are not quite ready to show in the Open A class. It contains a drop on recall in place of the Novice recall, and the long sit and long down are done with the owners out of sight.

Veteran is the Novice class for dogs that are at least seven years old. They can show here if they are old enough even if they have advanced titles. This class is mainly to give the old dog who can no longer clear the jumps of Open and Utility a class he can be retired to and still be active.

Brace is the Novice class for one handler with a pair of dogs that work shoulder to shoulder.

Team is Novice for four handlers and four dogs. They work simultaneously as a drill team. The drop on recall is added to the class.

Versatility is a class where two exercises are selected from each regular class: Novice, Open, and Utility. Each time a dog is shown in versatility, he may be called on to do different exercises.

In order to enter a show or obedience trial, you need to locate the show superintendent or the trial secretary at least a month and preferably six weeks before the show date. Entries for a show must be delivered before the entries close. The closing date is several weeks prior to the show to allow time to have the catalog printed. Kennel clubs put on dog shows and obedience trials but they usually hire a professional show superintendent to handle all the paperwork. The superintendent mails out premium lists that announce the show, list the awards, and contain entry blanks. The entries are sent back to the superintendent, who then has the catalogs printed, assembles the judges' books for recording the results, and is present at the show to administer it.

Obedience clubs put on independent obedience trials that have a small number of entries when compared to the thousands of dogs entered at an average dog show. Often a club member will be trial secretary and handle the entries. If you are new to the sport and want to be notified of such trials, you will need to drop a postcard to each club, requesting that they put you on their mailing list for future trials.

The quickest way to start receiving premium lists is to attend a dog show. While there, you need to do three things. First, ask the show superintendent to add you to his mailing list for at least the next six shows. Second, obtain copies of the premium lists that are on display. The superintendent will have stacks of premium lists available for his next several shows. He will be taking entries for those shows. Third, ask at the dog merchandise booths for a dog show calendar. It will be a yearly calendar with the shows in your area printed on it. It will identify the superintendent for each future show. Shop for your calendar. They vary little in price but considerably in quality. Ask someone at the show which one is the most accurate. Show people schedule their lives by these calendars. They will be happy to advise you about one. Calendar in hand, you then go home and write to the superintendents and trial secretaries whose events interest you. If this seems like a lot of effort, remember you only have to do it once. After you are on their mailing lists and have entered a few shows, you will receive premium lists virtually forever. One indication of a dog show person is a mailbox filled with premium lists. If all my premium lists were cancelled, the mailman would probably think I had moved out.

If you cannot reach a dog show for the direct approach, there are two other possibilities. If you know a person who shows dogs he probably receives as many premium lists as I do and would be happy to share them with you and provide you with superintendents' addresses. Dog show people generally believe that they can only be understood by other dog show people, and perhaps they are right. This makes them eager to expose a newcomer to the highly contagious condition known as dog show fever. One exposure is often enough to change a person's entire way of life.

If you cannot reach a dog show and do not know anyone who shows dogs, then the American Kennel Club will rescue you. This is a last resort because it takes longest. Write to the A.K.C. at 51 Madison Avenue, New York, N.Y. 10010. Request the superintendents' addresses and a subscription form to the *A.K.C. Gazette*, their official monthly magazine. It prints schedules of future events, results of the shows and obedience trials, and the names of all dogs that earn new titles. In addition there are bimonthly columns about each breed of dog and a variety of articles on every possible doggy subject. There is only one problem with subscribing to the *Gazette*—it is too useful a magazine to throw away. Each issue is the size of the telephone book for a small town. A year's worth of them is a stack more than a foot high. A five-year collection would be hundreds of pounds of magazines, and a twenty-year collection would probably weigh a ton. In a surprisingly short time you will find *Gazettes* lurking in every available storage corner—unless you are more resolute than I am and manage to throw them away.

Once you locate a trial that you want to enter and obtain a premium list for it, there are still a few more things to consider. Obedience trials are open to any purebred dog that is not blind or lame. Neutered dogs, monorchid and cryptorchid dogs, and dogs that have lost their pedigrees can be shown in obedience trials and tracking tests, although they cannot be shown in dog show breed classes.

How do you enter a dog that has no registration papers?

You obtain from the A.K.C. what is called an Indefinite Listing Privilege (I.L.P.) number. All the dog has to do is look like a member of some breed. You ask the A.K.C. for an application for an Indefinite Listing Privilege number. Fill out the application and return in it with a small filing fee and two photos of the dog. When they send you the I.L.P. number, the dog can compete at obedience trials and tracking tests where performance is being judged. Because the dog has no official pedigree he cannot be shown in breed competition, nor could his offspring be registered. For this reason I.L.P. dogs are seldom bred and are often altered.

Getting Into the Ring

Often the toughest part of any obedience trial is getting the dog into the ring at any given time. When an obedience steward says that you are next into the ring, it is a good idea to take that statement with a grain of salt. On one depressing day I was supposed to be next in the ring, but six dogs were shown ahead of me. Aside from being an example of poor manners and worse organization, why should it matter? It matters because a dog brought to the ring entrance to be shown should be alert and ready to show. Dogs that are taken into the ring half asleep tend to work that way. A number of things can be used to wake the dog up: an on leash recall, a short quick heeling pattern, or a couple of pivots at heel. Some dogs respond best to a few small pieces of liver given before they compete; just remember that food cannot be carried or offered to the dog in the ring. In warming a dog up, it is necessary to understand that there is a rule against drilling, or intensive or abusive training, of dogs on a show site. This rule was added to the regulations when there were complaints of dogs being abused at early trials.

Fifty feet of heeling is not drilling or intensive or abusive training. However, because of the confusion about this regulation, most exhibitors are intimidated into skulking off to little-used parts of the showgrounds to warm their dogs up privately. A favorite choice is just beyond the show boundary rope.

Once the dog is alert and ready at the ring entrance, the handler can only hope that he will be allowed to show at once. If the order is changed, and the dog has to sit around idle for another twenty minutes, he is going to go back to sleep. Even worse, if he is brought up to a ring-ready state repeatedly and the showing is postponed each time, he will become too bored to care about getting ready to show when it finally counts.

Checking Out the Ring

Some distractions in the ring can be prevented with a little observation and effort. It is possible to suggest to a family enjoying a smorgasbord lunch on the lawn at ringside that they might like to cover a few of the more tempting appetizers for the next few minutes or risk losing them. A German shepherd once ate a canapé from a ringside buffet table as he performed the retrieve over the high jump at the old Beverly Hills show. That was in the days when it was catered, and yes, the Shepherd did complete her retrieve. Her snack did not even slow her down much.

Double roped rings are nice. They hold the spectators several feet back from the dog and prevent them from dribbling popcorn on the dog's back. Actually, Sunny was never very fond of popcorn. What she was mad for were whole peanuts, which she would happily retrieve for me to shell out for her. Showing on a football field after a game, she tended to work from peanut to peanut.

If there are skateboarders playing just outside where the long-sit line is going to be, and the ring stewards do not remove them, the owner can do it. Just rush over before the group moves into the ring and suggest that the skateboards go elsewhere for the next ten minutes. You may need to show your teeth a little bit but it seems to work.

Many dogs in this day of plastic-wrapped dog food are readily attracted by the crinkle of cellophane. If your dog is one of these, and you see a ringside crinkler, a few kind words will usually get him to put it away for a little while.

It is always advisable to check the heights of the jumps. No one is perfect, and the jumps may end up the wrong height for your dog. The only time I have had to question a height was when they accidentally set up a forty-inch-high jump. The maximum allowable height is thirty-six inches. Greyhounds do jump well, but there are limits.

Many rings have poor surfaces. Grass rings may have holes, bare spots, dirt clods, or puddles, depending on the weather. Asphalt-surfaced rings may have eroded paving, cracks, and bumps.

Concrete rings can be wet and slick. Whatever the surface, you try the best you can to help the dog. In a grass ring it is not necessary to have the dog sit in the holes. If need be, the handler stands in the hole and gives the advantage to the dog. Some dogs will detour around bad footing, thereby putting little bulges in the heeling pattern. If the ring is paved with runners or carpet strips for the dogs, then give the dog the center of the runner to walk on. He needs it more than you do.

Dogs with prominent bones and thin skin will justifiably object to having to sit on a paved surface that pinches their skin between their hock bones and the pavement. It is possible to wear pressure sores clear through the skin on a large dog. This is something that no dog should have to tolerate in the name of sport.

You can help a dog pass the long sits and downs just by being a little careful about what you are making him lie on. As the line of dogs walks into the ring, check the ground. As you prepare to stop, it is nearly always possible to shift at least a dog's width in one direction or another. Pick a spot that you would like to lie on. If there is carpeting with wide tape fastening the seams together and you are in the sun, do not put a dog down with its belly on the tape. Tape reaches high temperatures in direct sunlight. At one show the lawn had been aerated, which left the ring covered with small dirt clods. It was easy to reach down and brush a small clear space in front of the dog. Instead of dropping into her usual sphinx position, she then lay flat on her side, giving me the delightful opportunity of watching her discover that her shoulder was on a collection of lumpy clods. During the three minutes of the down, she rolled her front upright, inch by inch. She was still not comfortable, and I was waiting for her to stand up to shift position and then lie down again. She fooled me. She gave a little hitch and moved from the hip lying position to a sphinx position without having risen. Finding herself safe in her little clod-free patch, she settled in to wait out the exercise.

Many large dogs sensibly will refuse to jump full height on poor footing. This is usually a problem on paved surfaces and it can be the result of the pavement's being either too smooth and slippery or too rough and abrasive. On bare cement the problem is usually slickness, and the least the owner can do is treat the bottom of the dog's feet with one of the commercial nonslip substances like Tacky Paw. If this is not available, an emergency substitute is to dip the bottom of the dog's feet in Coca Cola and let it partially dry. Trying to stuff a grown dog's feet in a Coke puddle at ringside is another of the unusual experiences that showing dogs leads to.

An excessively rough pavement is usually the result of old asphalt having been eroded away, and leaving the rock aggregate sticking up from the surface. Dogs may refuse to jump or sit or lie down on this pavement, and I don't blame them. The only solution is to protest to the host kennel club and to the A.K.C. until the conditions are improved. Showing should not be painful for the dog.

Cues and Body Language

The oldest and most advanced form of horsemanship is called dressage. The Spanish Riding School in Vienna uses Lippizan stallions to provide the best-known showcase for this art form.

In dressage the horse performs a series of intricate maneuvers without receiving any visible cues from its rider. The key word here is *visible*. The horse is receiving cues constantly, but they are so subtle that they are known only to the horse and rider. To the spectator, the rider appears to be motionless while the horse appears to be performing unaided. It may take from three to fifteen years for the horse and rider to reach this degree of subtlety.

Some dogs are born subtle. Others learn at their obedience classes. One of the problems in showing a well-trained dog is to avoid having it respond to unintentional cues that the owner may not even be aware of having given. There are three ways of accomplishing this goal. One is for the owner to develop such total body and expression control that he never gives inadvertent cues, but it produces a very stiff and dull performance and a rather stiff handler. The second is to teach the dog to ignore all the unintentional cues that the owner produces by punishing the dog whenever it does respond to one. This involves so much negative reinforcement—since each time the dog is being disciplined for trying to do what it thinks the owner wants—that the result is often a discouraged dog. The third choice is to learn what one's own secondary cues are and to use them to create a smooth and coordinated performance. The desired end result is similar to a dressage performance.

The dog, like any trained dog, is constantly responding to

nuances of its owner's behavior, but the only perceptible cues are those that are required to be given by the rules. Since there are two levels of communication taking place between the dog and handler, this leads us directly into an area of the obedience regulations that is subject to interpretation. What the regulations say is clear enough at one point. ". . . a single command or signal only may be given by the handler, and any extra commands or signals must be penalized." This would appear to apply to the formal commands designated by the regulations. In other words, if a handler gives a dog an extra "Heel" cue where it is not called for, he will lose points for it. Such recourse to an extra cue would be superior to allowing the dog to wander off and fail the exercise.

Farther down the section on Commands and Signals, things become more complicated. The paragraph starts out with a sentence that has always baffled me: "Signaling correction to a dog is forbidden and must be penalized." This seems quite straightforward, but the problem is, how does one signal correction to a dog? The word "correction" in the regulations is generally used to mean discipline. I do not have a signal that disciplines a dog, nor does anyone else whom I have watched show. Saying "Ick poo, rotten puppy," does not qualify as a signal, no matter how the owner feels. Perhaps this is the one instance in the regulations where correction is meant the way I use it, that is, cueing a dog from one activity to a different, desired one. If this is what it means, it would be possible to signal corrections to a dog that was facing the wrong glove on the directed retrieve or was about to pick up the wrong scent article. Doing so in either case would fail the dog, as the handler is allowed only one command for these exercises. This leaves the sentence about signaling correction purposeless, whichever way you care to interpret the word "correction."

It is nice that the next sentence in the regulations is clear cut. "Signals must be inaudible and the handler must not touch the dog." In other words, if a handler chooses to heel with hand signals, he is not allowed to clap his hands for the signal nor to hold the dog's ear. Having gone from the obscure to the explicit, the regulations then move into an area subject to interpretation, with: "Any unusual noise or motion may be considered to be a signal. Movements of the body that aid the dog shall be considered additional signals. . . ." Each of these sentences raises its own questions. What is an unusual noise or motion? And since most body movements affect the dog, which ones should be considered additional signals? This is an area of interpretation that each judge and each exhibitor has to sort out for himself. The exhibitor can fall back on the judge's responsibility and say that any cues the judge does not object to and penalize are allowable. I would like to take a more charitable view, however. Since obedience is a sport, it does help to observe standards of good sportsmanship. This means that each exhibitor has the opportunity to decide for himself where the boundary is between normal body language and additional signals.

In the end it comes down to a choice of personal conscience. I have a Novice bitch that does totally reliable group exercises. She would rather sit than stand and rather lie than sit. Immobility is her idea of fun. You can imagine my surprise at her first trial when on the long sit she started slowly to walk her front out, getting ready to lie down. Not caring to watch her go down by inches, I turned my head and watched collies being judged in an adjoining ring. When I looked back, expecting to see her down, she was sitting sort of at half mast intently watching the collie ring. Apparently she had decided that if I thought there was something worth seeing there it would be worth her attention. The first time it happened was accidental, but it turned out that looking away from her was a reliable method of steadying her group exercises. As the bottom member of the pack, she grew nervous when I, as pack leader, stared at her intently during a group exercise. To dogs, that kind of fixed stare is a challenge, and she literally could not face it. But was looking back over my shoulder an extra signal once I knew how she would respond to it?

Or to use another instance, we once showed in Open for a judge who had the jump in the center of the ring with the broad jump next to it. They are usually on opposite sides of the ring. Sunny cleared the broad jump, turned to come back to me, and froze as she saw the judge and me standing on opposite edges of the high jump. The correction for running around the high jump is to be met by someone beside it. I could see her trying to sort out what was happening. Was she supposed to come to me to finish the broad jump exercise or was she in trouble somehow for not jumping the high jump? She looked from it to me. I smiled until my face felt stiff, then relaxed, because a fixed smile loses its effect, and smiled once again. Sunny was reassured and came in to sit in front. The judge said jokingly, "I should penalize you for facial signals." She was kidding, but had she chosen to, it would have been fine with me.

The job of the handler is to get the dog to perform the exercises correctly. It is the responsibility of the judge to make whatever deductions from a perfect score he feels are justified.

What To Do While Failing

"He has failed at three straight trials, and he is such a good working dog," sniffled the handsome young man with the very handsome Belgian shepherd.

"What does he do?" I inquired solicitously.

"He only comes halfway in on the recall and then he sits."

"Every time?"

"At three straight shows."

"What do you do when he sits? Do you call him again right away?"

"I wait until the judge tells me to call him."

The young man had three separate problems: 1) finding out what caused the dog to make its first mistake; 2) the fact that the mistake was fast becoming a habit; 3) not knowing how to help the dog once it had failed.

The most common reason for a dog to sit out of the handler's reach is that most handlers are so tense about being in competition that they look at the dog with terrifying desperation. That is, the owner is desperate. The dog is dubious. I badly wanted to have a series of photos of typical ring expressions, but most people understandably are reluctant to have unflattering photos published. Ninety percent of the out-of-reach sits could be avoided by a smile.

Once the Belgian had sat out of reach at the first show, the owner was even more tense at the next one, and the dog sat out of reach again. Besides, by this time he was getting the hang of it. Sitting out of reach was what he was supposed to do at obedience trials. This production of a bad habit within the show ring is something that the experienced handler tries to avoid at all costs. Few things are more frustrating than the ringwise dog, the dog who knows that the one place in the world where he does not have to obey is in the obedience ring. Dogs quickly learn that the regulations forbid corrections or training in the ring.

What should the handler do as the dog fails an exercise? If the dog is still in position to perform the exercise, he should be given an immediate verbal second command, which is usually all that is needed to have him complete the exercise. A second command is not training in the ring. It is just an extra command. It will lead to a zero score on some exercises but it is only used if the dog has zeroed anyway. It insures that the dog successfully completes the exercise and prevents the formation of the habit of failure. The exercises that are particularly helped by repeating the cue are the recall, the retrieve, the signal exercise, and the scent discrimination, if the dog is declining to bring an article. If the dog brings the wrong article, you pretend that it really is the right one. After all, he did retrieve, and you do not want to discourage that, but then do additional training on scent discrimination exercises before the next trial. Failures in the group exercises are accepted as indicating a need for more training, more exposure to distractions, or perhaps a need for a few practice matches where corrections would be permitted.

The moment that a dog fails an exercise at an obedience trial, the handler's concern is to do whatever he can for the rest of the ring routine to make the dog perform better at the *next* trial. As soon as a dog nonqualifies, the trial becomes a practice match. While you cannot correct a dog at a trial, you can call to it, praise it, and if necessary talk it through the remaining exercises.

Never Fail Heeling

There are two main ways to fail an off leash heeling exercise. The first is to have the dog say, "The heck with this," and leave the ring. The more common way is for the dog to stop in his tracks and stare wistfully after the departing owner. Once the owner is several feet away from the dog, the dog decides that it must really be a stay exercise and he stays in place and fails. What never seems to happen is for the owner to realize that he is losing the dog and to say once again, "Dog, heel." The additional heeling cue is points off, not nonqualifying. Not knowing this, most owners just walk away from their dog. I did it myself once as a novice and know how it feels, which may be why I hate to see anyone else in the same situation. What happens when you walk away from a dog that is heeling in the ring is that you are teaching him to freeze during the heeling pattern when he is shown. This can set up a pattern that is difficult to break.

The Handicap

Working as a ring clerk at an obedience trial turned out to be an unexpectedly fascinating and educational experience. I had thought that it would be like the practice matches I had helped at periodically. It was not. The dogs quickly learn the difference between a match and a trial. The difference is that corrections can be made at a match while they are not allowed at a trial. The dogs that have learned this rule perform quite meticulously at a match and save their inventiveness for real trials, where anything goes. At this trial, there was the doberman and his handler who heeled like square-dance partners, performing a do-si-do at each turn as dog and owner would turn in opposite directions. Then the dog would make a full circle and run to catch up to his receding owner. They were quickly followed by a cocker spaniel that ended the recall by throwing himself flat on the ground with his head buried between the owner's ankles. Our ring help was mesmerized by a handicapped lady in the adjoining ring working Novice very competently in a motorized wheelchair. We admired her determination and skill as she maneuvered the balky wheelchair over the bumpy grass of her ring. She passed the individual exercises with her sheltie after a dismaying moment when it looked as if her battery had died. But the power came back and she finished the class. Then we turned to find that our next exhibitor was another motorized handler. Before the class was over he would teach us some things about ourselves.

The quest for the appearance of physical perfection reaches a fever pitch of intensity in dog breeding and dog shows. The unfit and imperfect are culled, and it is denied that they ever existed. With all this emphasis on physical attributes, one might expect the owners and handlers to be avid believers in physical culture for themselves as well as their dogs. It is easier to own perfection than it is to achieve it. The most beautiful Collie Champion that I have met was owned and

A truly willing dog will heel off lead as well as he does on a lead. Once a dog is well trained for heeling you should be able to talk him through the exercise. Practice pure incentive free heeling and you will learn whether you have a happy dog or just one that respects the leash.

loved by a gentleman with a spinal deformity. I have always been fascinated by the attraction that the tall, skinny sighthounds have for ladies of exactly the opposite body type. It still makes me flinch to watch a handler, who has run to show five consecutive dogs in widely separated rings, pant up to the sixth ring and, on finding that he has time before the next dog, light a cigarette. I keep waiting for this kind of handler to drop at my feet in a heart attack. No matter that show folk do not believe in fitness for themselves, they still insist on it for those around them. Thus a severe handicap tends to stimulate the response of, "Gee, that is too bad. They should have culled that one." It is a bit discomforting to find that you are applying that line of thought to a person.

Our exhibitor was a cerebral palsy victim. The resulting impairment of physical coordination prevented him from holding the leash or working the collar snap, so his friend requested that I remove the leash for the off-lead exercises. For the on-lead heeling it was looped over the arm of a wheelchair. Cerebral palsy also produces a speech impediment. At first his speech was unintelligible to us because we *did not listen*. We could not understand him because we *assumed* that we could not, and therefore did not make the effort to pay close attention. By the end of the class we had learned to understand him. We had also learned that he was a trainer, not a cripple, and one of us. When we could stop looking past him and patronizing him out of our embarrassment, he became a person to us, and one with some worthwhile insights into dog training.

But we did not know that to begin with. At the start he was just a fascinating example of an obedience trainer overcoming unusual obstacles. We watched him through the on-leash heeling, the yellow Labrador Retriever tied to the wheelchair with a faith stronger than the leash. The figure eight was a bit exciting as he struggled to persuade the balky wheelchair to follow the necessary figure without running down one of the ring clerks. For a moment I expected to be the obedience ring's first wheelchair casualty, but he corrected course and finished the exercise. As I removed the Labrador's leash, her owner was breathing like a sprinter after a one-hundred-yard dash. He later said that the figure eight was the most difficult exercise, not for the dog, but for the handler and wheelchair. In the stand for examination, as he returned to the dog, an erratic twitch of the wheelchair almost brought it up against her, but she stood without flinching while her owner backed off and came to the correct heel position. The dog was incredibly steady throughout the class. The free heeling and recall were no problem. The handler had passed the individual exercises and was transported with joy. Then the ring help could relax from the strain of *willing* the dog to qualify.

The group exercises followed immediately, with the wheelchair handler on the end of the line to give him maneuvering room. I took the leash again and backed off ten feet to watch half of the dogs for the long sit. Almost immediately the Labrador, who had been so steady and imperturbable, began to walk her front out—that is, to step forward with her front feet while leaving her rump on the ground. There was a sudden increase in tension in the ring because this maneuver usually results in the dog's gradually lying down. Many dogs will stretch their front feet out a few steps to check to see if it is safe to lie down. When the owner does not respond to the movement—and at a trial he cannot respond—the dog knows that corrections are not allowed. It then settles down for a nap.

I assumed that her owner would not have recourse to the little strategems that experienced handlers know, those things that the judges refer to as the "Long-sit-sneeze," and the "Long-down-cough." These are non-dogtraining actions that pull a dog's wandering attention back to his owner.

Anything that draws a dog's attention can steady the group exercises. Tiger held the long sit for his third C.D.X. leg in plus-hundred-degree weather because the breed exhibitors came over to watch him. You could see his attention fix on the greyhounds arriving outside the ring. He was so fascinated by them that he forgot to nap.

Certain that the handicapped handler would be without ring subterfuges, I ran through one of my old ones. The dog stopped where she was momentarily, and I was waiting for the next move when her attention suddenly fixed on her handler and she held her position for the rest of the time. The ring steward, the handler, and the judge all heaved a sigh of relief. The down was easy and she had qualified. As I attached her leash and snapped her back to the wheelchair, her owner was ecstatic. It had been a cliff-hanger, and those are really the most fun to win. It had also been her third leg in three trials. I wanted to congratulate him but patronized him instead. After all that I have written about obedience for fun, and the value of playtraining, I assumed that he would not understand that and complimented him instead on the work that he must have put into his training. He wasn't about to be patronized, and his answer brought me up short. He said, "No. It was not work. If it had been work I wouldn't have done it. It was fun." Which is what I have been trying to explain. Ultimately, obedience is not taught because the dog refuses to come or it will not lie down. Obedience is taught because it is *fun*.

By this time the owner had my attention, and I was easily understanding what he was saying. Once outside the ring he had one more surprise in store. Not quite having learned my lesson yet, I tried to explain to him about the existence of ring aids like the long-sit-sneeze. He said, "Oh, yes, everybody has them. I was using mine when she almost went down." Then he reached out to toy with the toggle switch that controlled the wheelchair, and the dog came alert just as she had in the ring. She had learned to associate the sound of the switch with motion. I suddenly remembered that the dogs of both wheelchair handlers responded to the sound of the switch and motor. So I wished him well, and he rolled away. He certainly didn't need either my advice or sympathy. All he needed was to be treated as a person instead of an invalid or a stereotype.

The Wheelchair's Revenge

Although I had met the wheelchair handler, none of my dogs had ever seen him until I took Kitty Hawk to a two-day out-of-state circuit. We were just starting the long sit, with the dogs on one side of the ring and the handlers on the other, when Kitty Hawk's head snapped around to the left and her eyes widened. Rolling around the end of the ring and along behind the line of dogs came my friend in his motorized wheelchair. At moments like this you try telepathy or possibly it is prayer. In any event it worked. The handler noticed the line of dogs and possibly the Hawk's alarm and stopped ten feet short of her. What I knew, and he did not, is that the Hawk has an unusually long fight-flight distance, and he was within it. First she turned her head away to avoid looking at him and lay down in an ostrich head-in-the-sand type of maneuver. I was surprised (I expected her to get up and bolt), but it was somewhat reassuring. There was at least a chance that she might hold the down. We repositioned our dogs for the long down and left them. There was a small noise from the wheelchair, and the Hawk did what I had been waiting for all along, leapt to her feet and stood there staring nervously back over her shoulder at the wheelchair as if it were the world's largest skateboard come to chase her. There was a good chance she would hold her position, but if she did move away from the wheelchair she would move directly over the sheltie on her right, and I could hear the sheltie owner's breath tighten next to me. There was not any point in risking someone else's score, so I quietly called Kitty Hawk out of line. It felt rather odd. I had never called a dog out of a group exercise before. It is one of those taboos. And it was a relief to find that the sky did not fall in. She walked with dignity across the ring, let me put an arm around her, and continued to look mistrustfully at the offending wheelchair.

That still left the question of how would she perform under the same circumstances the next day. As we left the ring, I took her to meet the handler and his wheelchair. We talked for a while, and I learned that he was there to show for the first time in Open. His yellow Labrador Retriever still looked as steady and reliable as ever. As he left to get ready, I followed along with Kitty Hawk to let her become used to the sound of the running motor.

The next morning as we lined up to do the group exercise in Novice B, who should come wheeling in but my friend and his Lab, who were to work just then in the next ring.

I was distressed. "Why two days in a row?" But Kitty Hawk never bothered to look their way and did as well in the group exercise as any dog can. The moral: Dogs accept handicaps more quickly than people do, but they need a chance to recover from the initial strangeness. Find a wheelchair and follow it around for a bit. Let the dog set its own pace. Never force a dog close to something it is afraid of. Doing so simply reinforces its fears. If you act as if nothing is unusual, the dog will quickly accept it.

Why Do Obedience People Dress Like That? (Sloppily)

It is possible to wear almost anything in the Obedience ring, and I probably have. Having outgrown an early Levi's period, I look back on it in some puzzlement. I was wearing in the ring the same things that I was wearing to train the dogs, on the peculiar assumption that they might be bothered by a change in wardrobe styles. Lurking in the back of my mind was the possibility that the dogs might not recognize me in a dress. When we started to show in the breed rings, which are more formal, the wardrobe changed. The dogs were not bothered.

An incident at a show in San Diego changed my outlook on dressing for obedience. I had entered both an obedience dog and a breed dog. In the breed ring the competing handlers would be two of the most attractive and best dressed men in the dog show world. One was a former actor-turned-doctor who has a preference for elegant Italian three-piece suits. The other was the prettiest male professional handler in the country. Deciding that my dog and I might be outshown, but that I would not be outdressed, I put as much effort into my own grooming as always goes into the dog's grooming. Win, lose, or draw, the Greyhound ring was going to be a scene of sartorial splendor. The schedule that day required that the obedience dog be shown first. It was the worst ring surface I have ever seen, old bare asphalt with the rock edges exposed. It was like asking a dog to work on crushed glass.

If I had realized in time how bad it was, we would not have shown. Kitty Hawk worked the Novice class with growing reluctance and left the ring with both hocks bleeding from asphalt abrasions. She had worked as well as she could under the circumstances, but I was irritated with the show committee for allowing such poor ring conditions. Suddenly a young couple came up, all smiles, to say how nice Kitty Hawk and I had looked in the ring. I was grateful, but puzzled. Usually a compliment on an obedience performance means that the dog has worked well, and Kitty Hawk had not. Then I realized that the words were meant literally. Kitty Hawk is a flashy attractive Greyhound, and I was turned out for the fashion show that was about to take place in the breed ring. The young couple were not obedience competitors and did not care about the fine points of ring performance. They were pleased by our decorative qualities. Appearance may not matter at all to the dog, and only slightly to the owner and the judge, but it does matter greatly to the spectators. Since obedience is supposed to demonstrate the usefulness of purebred dogs as companions, let us put on the best possible demonstration to the public. They do not have to believe that obedience is made up mainly of owners who look like they are dressed to clean out their garages, and of dogs that are so poorly bred or groomed as to be barely recognizable as purebred dogs. Care in dressing not only shows pride in your dog and your sport but there is an even more important reason for trying it, at least once: It is fun. It also puts some welcome showmanship into the obedience rings.

Just as showmanship can help in the obedience ring, some obedience can help in the show ring. At this show it made the difference between winning and losing. The breed ring conditions turned out to be different from those of the obedience ring, but just as poor. Instead of rough asphalt to hurt the dogs, there was slick concrete for them to slip on. Instead of cars being driven right by the edge of the ring, there were hordes of people and dogs packed around the ring area inside a warehouselike exhibit building. Walking through the doorway was like walking into a wall of noise. It was enough to make me flinch.

Our class entered the ring, looking like a competition for best-dressed handler. The racket and confusion completely distracted one of the dogs. The dog I was showing had seen a lot of racket and confusion in his life with me. We deliberately go out in search of it for training purposes. Besides that, he had faith that his pack leader (me) would not let anything nasty happen to him, so he showed as if there were nothing unusual about the conditions. It was just the edge he needed to win that day.

Heat

People and horses can remain active in hot weather because both have the ability to sweat. The evaporation of perspiration is one of the most efficient ways possible of ejecting body heat. Dogs lack this ability, and this leads them to dig holes in the ground, both to reach cool earth levels and to create shade. They also sleep out the warm part of the day in the shade. When we take them to an obedience trial in warm weather, it becomes our responsibility to keep them comfortable. This means providing shade, drinking water, and artificial sweat in the form of a spray bottle full of water. The dog is kept damp, like a load of laundry waiting to be ironed. For the judge's sake it is considerate to leave a dry strip down the center of the dog's back for the stand for examination. The idea is to wet down the parts of the body that have large blood supplies: the top of the head, the ears, the throat, the underbelly, and, on a male dog, the testicles. The best way to keep a dog comfortable is to consider the probable temperatures at a given show before you enter it, and avoid those shows that are predictably hot.

Love and Disappointment

No dog works spectacularly all the time. To all dogs there eventually comes an off day. When this happens in the ring, the owner is often affected strangely. It is not at all uncommon to see an owner showing disappointment in the ring. The owner's rejection of the dog can reach a point where it seems that they are a pair of strangers that somehow ended up in the ring together by accident. The owner is salvaging his own pride by playing to the sympathy of the audience and the judge, and is punishing the dog for working poorly by rejecting him. The problem here is that the more the dog is rejected, the worse he is going to work, both for the rest of the day and very likely in the future. A dog that is having problems needs help, not rejection. He needs additional cues. He needs intensified praise and encouragement at the very time when it is the hardest to give. At this point we find out if the owner is worthy of the dog. It is easy to love a dog that is performing well. To feel virtuous, most people can bring themselves to say that they love their dog even though it is not working well just now. But this is still conditional love, dependent on the dog's performance or the owner's forgiveness. The ultimate goal is to make love unconditional, to be able to give two separate, unrelated statements of fact and not to have one dependent on the other. Thus: "I love the dog." "The dog is working poorly (or well) today." The two statements have nothing to do with each other, and once the owner truly believes it he will never be disappointed again in a ring performance. The resulting sense of optimism and freedom it gives is amazing. If you love the dog before you take him into the ring, you can love him just as much when you leave the ring. The choice is yours, but I recommend it.

Flaws. Nothing is perfect, neither dogs nor dog sports. They all have some faults. Three problems in obedience are the boredom of most trials, the zeal of a few judges, and the attitude of what seems to be an increasing number of exhibitors.

The Trial

To the novice exhibitor the average obedience trial is incredibly dull because of the normal slow exhibition pace and the lack of a clear-cut judging time. I vividly recall my very first trial. It took four hours to show two dogs. I watched the rings, read most of a paperback, and went home thinking, "How can all those people possibly do that for fun? What an incredible bore!" As it turned out, what the regular obedience exhibitors do during the waiting time is to renew old acquaintances, catch up on the grapevine news, and just plain visit and socialize. By the next trial I was no longer a stranger, and I never did manage to read another book while waiting. So the tedium of the trial is a problem that solves itself as one's circle of friends expands. The time-consuming routine of an obedience trial is just a bit of an initial shock to the breed exhibitor who is used to bouncing into the ring at the scheduled time and then being through and ready to go home a half hour later.

The Exhibitors

The problem with the minority of exhibitors who become hyper-competitors is that they lose sight of the basic purpose of obedience trials. Many of these fanatic obedience addicts believe that the purpose of obedience trials is to give the contestants a place to earn obedience titles, obedience championships, *Dog World* (Will Judy) awards, and places in the year's top-ten dog standings. None of these competitive facets of obedience is its main purpose. The actual purpose is stated with admirable clarity in what seems to be the most neglected portion of the A.K.C. *Obedience Regulations*. "Purpose" has its own section in the regulations, the very first and perhaps least-read section in all the regulations. It should be read more often, because this section contains four of the most important statements to be found anywhere in the pamphlet. The first is *"The purpose of obedience trials is to demonstrate the usefulness of the pure-bred dog as a companion of man . . ."* There it is, folks. There is no mention of 200-point scores, or High in Trial winners, or even competition. Obedience trials are a *demonstration* of the dog's usefulness, not an arena in which to satisfy the owner's competitive instincts. The handy Webster's dictionary can help us resolve any confusion as to the difference between the two aspects. A demonstration is a "display" of the dog's abilities. By comparison the definition of competition is "a contest between two rivals." Unfortunately, for a persistent number of entrants, obedience seems to be more a contest than a demonstration.

The Arena. So what is the matter with having obedience become a contest? The basic drawback is that in any contest there are a few winners and many losers, and both suffer in the long run. The winners develop an addiction to winning that often amounts to a fanatic drive. The losers are disappointed in themselves and in their dogs. The problem with both reactions is that they damage the relationship between the dog and its owner. The winner, in pursuit of future wins, becomes able to self-justify doing quite unfriendly things to the dog. If he succeeds, then he shows until the inevitable day that the dog retires. Often the successful dog is shown long after he should retire, after he has lost all enthusiasm for, and even the physical ability to, perform the exercises. When he finally does retire, the owner is faced with the task of training as a replacement a dog that generally has less natural aptitude than the decrepit superdog. This is especially true because many owners are introduced to obedience by one dog of exceptional natural Novice talent. They take Woofles to the local dog class and, at the end of the class, the trainer says "Hey, that is a good working dog. Why don't you show him next month?" So they take him to the show. He does well and they are hooked on the sport. There are two kinds of good working dogs, the ones you raise from scratch and do not make too many mistakes with, and the ones you just blunder across. Either kind is nice to have, but once the owner knows how to start with a puppy and create a good working dog, he can repeat the process for the next dog.

The saddest thing that happens to some winning dogs is that they become depersonalized. They become a means to an end, a part of the owner's fantasy life. If the owner did not have the illusion of "winning" to cloud his vision, he would be able to see when the dog was ready to retire. He would be able to see the new dog as an individual instead of as the tool of his sport. The critical question is, "If dog shows and trials were abolished tomorrow, would one's dog population change?" There is a difference between keeping a dog for the pleasure of its company and showing it for entertainment and keeping the dog as a basic piece of sport's equipment. The dog deserves the former.

The dogs would prefer to sleep more comfortably at home.

Losing is far less addictive than winning, not surprisingly, since few people set out to become attached to losing. It is true that some people do become chronic losers, but that is a separate problem. The short-term result of losing is to cause the owner to be unhappy with himself and the dog. It is hardly fair to blame the dog, since the owner, not the dog, is responsible for the training. The owner has entered and driven to the trial. The dog would probably prefer to be asleep at home. Reducing the owner's self-esteem is both unpleasant and pointless. No one but you *cares* about how you place in a trial. Why then punish yourself for an off day's performance? In the larger sense, why punish yourself for anything? It is a leftover habit from our childhood days when we were rewarded by grown-ups for being good (this is winning) and punished when we were bad (their value judgment, not ours). A fascinating aspect of human behavior is that as we grow up and the grown-ups disappear (they disappear because we become them), we carefully store away the old habits and, in the absence of anyone else to do it to us, we punish ourselves for losing, or being wrong, or being bad.

In this process we become so entrapped in hopes for the future and recollections of past triumphs and disasters that we lose the ability to do what dogs and children are good at, to *live in and feel the present*. To experience wonder and curiosity and to *feel* what is happening to us right now. Most sports focus on a moment that requires such immediate concentration that we are forced temporarily to shed our well-worn pasts and well-rehearsed tomorrows and to live for an instant in the present. Whether the sport is powder skiing or jumping horses, river running or acrobatic flying, the attraction of these high-speed activities is not, as is commonly thought, their element of risk. The attraction is that the speed and degree of risk *forces* total concentration on the activity and this compels the participant to live momentarily in the present time. It frees him of the baggage of past memories and future fantasies that litter our everyday minds and compete with the present for our attention. Acting in present time is the key to concentration and excellence in any sport. It is only when we are thinking in the present that we can learn anything, since learning can only be felt in the present. A good golf swing, target shot, sprint, artwork, or seduction are all done in present time. More importantly *good* dog training is done in present time. Nothing exists for the trainer except himself, the dog, and their communication. At this point training becomes play and an end in itself instead of just homework to be done as a means to a secondary end, that end being showing. As long as the trainer keeps his priorities in order and remembers that he and the dog come first and that the trial is a subordinate activity, the results of a show performance will not be allowed to affect the friendship between the dog and owner.

Winners and Losers

The winners and losers at a trial are both losers when they allow competition to interfere with their feelings about the dog. Each trial day, indeed each day of life, is unique. It is the only twenty-four hours available to the dog and owner that day. It is this gift of time that is ultimately the most precious of all. If the owner allows considerations of losing to spoil that day then he is, indeed, the final loser.

The morning of a dog show, or obedience trial or lure course is a very special and almost magical time. It is also a bit difficult to explain to nonexhibitors. The cold facts of the activities—that one is getting up at 5 A.M. in order to drive two hundred miles to a dog show—can be relied on to elicit sympathy from even the sternest listener. A little sympathy is always welcome, so why should we tell them that we do not deserve the sympathy, that those early mornings are fun? First there is the satisfaction of rising early enough to wake the dogs up for a change, instead of their acting as our most reliable alarm clocks. A call brings them, sleepy-eyed, out of their doghouses to yawn and stretch in disbelief at the surrounding darkness. Then a transformation takes place as they realize from the early hour that it must be a dog event day, and they change from reluctant risers to a wildly excited pack. No one wants to be left behind, as they each entreat, "Take me." "Take ME!" "TAKE ME." "TAKE US ALL." So the traveling dogs are selected and the stay-at-home dogs are fed in consolation. They are the only ones to enjoy breakfast. While I am a person who on normal mornings cannot even speak civily until after a sizable breakfast, on show mornings food is entirely dispensable. Freshwater containers and ice are loaded into the car, which was packed the previous night. Finally, the dogs are tucked in and we are off. After the excitement of the departure the dogs promptly go to sleep. That is, Sunny goes to sleep in the back. Tiger rides in the passenger seat with his head in my lap. He has logged sixty-thousand miles, and on each trip he still rouses intermittently from his dozing to check on our progress. After a quick look around, he drops his head back onto my knee where it has rested through a thousand hours of similar drives. The thing I was the most grateful for when he finished his championship was never again to have to put up with the show-clipped chin whiskers prickling against my leg. Ick! While Tiger naps and watches for our destination, Sunny snores contentedly behind us.

There is a saying to the effect that dog-show folk never get to Heaven because they are at a dog show every Sunday and therefore never attend church. Even so we are not out of touch with religion. Secure in our cars, alone on an empty freeway, watching the sunrise of one more silver dawn, we have the opportunity to listen to an unbroken string of radio evangelists. They follow each other at half-hour intervals. With each station break, deep Southern drawls replace Midwest twangs, only to be replaced in turn by homogenized Southern Californisms. A virtual smorgasbord of religious persuasion keeps us company on those long, lonesome highways that seem so strangely free of cars, and are somehow also free of worries and everyday distractions. It is the start of a new day when anything is possible, and dreams of Best in Shows, or High in Trials, or Best in Fields rest gently with us. We can entertain them for what they are, fantasies and hopes for the future, with the acknowledgment that, although the odds may be long against us, there is always the possibility of the ultimate win. Puppies do win Best in Show, and Novice A dogs do win High in Trial. When we have cherished and played with our fantasies, we can move on to the more attainable hopes of qualifying in obedience or taking the points in breed.

The outcome of the day's activities does not matter to the dog. Only you and your opinion of him matter to the dog. When we first began to show, we started a little ritual that went with the morning drive. It consisted of pats for each dog and a single sentence. "For any weird and wonderful thing that you choose to do to me in the ring today, I forgive you now." The ritual may not have helped the dogs, but it did wonders for relieving the owner's tensions, and for keeping our goals in perspective. Just one thing—for it to work you have to truly mean it.

Goals and Aspiration

There is a second dog-eared saying that maintains that every dog except one is eventually a loser at a show. This is because of the pyramidal nature of the competition, where dogs are progressively eliminated until finally only the Best in Show or High in Trial dog remains undefeated (for that day). This is a depressing way of looking at the structure, and it ignores one vital point. Within a show or trial there are many levels of accomplishment available to each dog and owner. It is the owner who selects the goal for that day's competition: 200 points is a perfect obedience score; 170 points is a barely passing score. I have seen owners bitterly disappointed with 194.5 scores, and also owners who were ecstatic over scores of 172 or 178. The first owners had missed their self-set goals, while the happy owners had achieved theirs. How can we each avoid the winning-losing trap? It can be done only by coming to an understanding of ourselves and what our individual goals are. The range of goals is broader than just those that can be achieved at a dog show or trial. It is important that these be our *own* goals and not those leftover goals trained into us as children and still operating for us, as useless as an appendix. We must be careful that they are not the goals of other club members or fellow dog owners. We must know what we, personally, want in a relationship before we can deliberately create it. This is true whether it is applied to people or other animals. Most training is done in relationships established haphazardly because we do not make the effort to recognize our desires and act on them. Without that recognition we go through life reacting to outside influences instead of creating what we seek.

What do you want of your relationship with your dog and what price are you willing to pay for it? Try placing ranking numerical priorities (1-12) on each question of the following list:

_____ A. Do you want a High in Trial Dog?

_____ B. Do you want an Obedience Trial Champion?

_____ C. Do you want titles, whether C.D., C.D.X., or U.D.?

_____ D. Do you crave someday to win a runoff with a sheltie?

_____ E. Do you prefer a methodical, precise worker?

_____ F. Do you want a dog with high average scores?

_____ G. Do you want a dog with a high percentage of qualifications? (F and G often do not go together.)

_____ H. Do you want to improve your communication with and understanding of the dog?

_____ I. Do you want to be pleased with your effect on the development of the dog's personality?

_____ J. Do you want a dog that enters the ring bouncing and leaves it smiling?

_____ K. Do you want a dog with obedience, show, *and* field trial titles?

_____ L. Do you want an outgoing, enthusiastic, self-confident dog?

You would probably like to have all of the above. The purpose of ranking them from one through twelve is to find out which ones you really want the most, and the least. This kind of ranking can also be used for evaluating a group of nondog goals. Writing down the goals is not usually difficult; it is the assigning of numerical values to determine what you want most that is revealing. It helps us to communicate with ourselves. In looking at the completed ranking above, people of highly competitive persuasion are likely to find items A thru F high on their standings. These are where their emotional rewards come from and therefore these are the goals they should strive for. I do not condemn competitiveness in other people as long as they reread the Purpose section of the obedience regulations annually and keep in mind the very first sentence: "Obedience trials are a sport, and all participants should be guided by the principles of good sportsmanship both in and outside of the ring."

I do want to make space for those people whose primary interest is in the development and performance of the well-adjusted exuberant, confident, willing companion dog and who attend trials to exhibit the results of this type of training as opposed to simply competing for awards. Awards are singularly cold, hard objects. They will not snuggle up to you on a chill day or lick your hand when you sweat. The hope is to bring the emphasis off the trophy table and back to the dog, who deserves it.

A curious aspect of priorities is that they change with time. My current priorities are H, I, L, K, J, G, C, F, A, B, D, E in descending order. That listing would indicate a person to whom the quality of the dog-person friendship and the adventures in molding the personality of a growing puppy matter very much, while the value of competition slides down the list. A few years ago my ratings for competition would have been much higher. Items H through J would not even have been thought of. Good training teaches the trainer more than it teaches the dog, until, for many trainers, the competition aspects become unimportant. My current in-training dog is a delight. If she never sets paw in a ring, I will be satisfied with our progress, because the important part was what she taught me. There comes a time when you know that you have succeeded without needing the reinforcement of outside judges.

Judging the Judges

To the exhibitor, obedience judges seem to be omnipotent authorities on the sport of obedience. Seen from a distance they are often considered to be a homogeneous group. They appear to be totally interchangeable. Such stereotyping is an error with any group of people or dogs. Each one is a unique individual, and it helps to keep that in mind. What many obedience judges do have in common is that they are well-intentioned, hardworking, and underpaid when compared to breed judges. They also have firm opinions on the sport of obedience. All that the usual exhibitor wants to know about a judge is whether he is a tough or an easy scorer. It is often considerably more important to know how a particular judge interprets the A.K.C. obedience regulations and whether he follows the A.K.C.'s *Guidelines for Obedience Judges*.

The A.K.C. obedience regulations are written in general terms and are not detailed enough to determine a dog's score. Like breed standards, the regulations are subject to interpretation by each judge and exhibitor. However, the judge's interpretation is the only one that counts for the record. Just as the manner in which breed judges interpret a breed standard can shape a breed and direct a breeder's efforts, so the collective interpretation of the obedience regulations by the obedience judge molds the sport and directs trainers' efforts.

The majority of the judges do their best to interpret the rules in the light of common sense, and this is all that any exhibitor can ask. Unfortunately, a small minority of judges seem to have different criteria for interpreting the rules, and we will consider those next.

Judging Peculiarities

If you watch and participate in enough obedience trials, you are going to see some strange and unusual interpretations of the rules. About the only thing that all judges seem to agree on is that a crooked sit deserves a deduction of from one half to one full point. Scoring aside, one would expect it to be easy to tell if a dog had nonqualified on an exercise. It is not. Many judges will deduct minor points should a dog lie down during the long-sit *after* the time limit has been reached and the handlers are returning. Some judges will fail the dog for the same action. We might expect that a drop in the *middle* of the long-sit exercises would fail a dog. For at least one shepherd on at least one occasion, it has not. And when the owner, a lady who believed in playing strictly by the rules, suggested to the judge that her dog should not qualify, the judge was offended because she had questioned his judgment.

Generally, if a dog knocks the bar off the bar jump, the dog will not qualify. But then it might, because judges differ, and some will pass the dog. The rules are quite explicit about the necessity of excusing from the ring a lame dog. Yet at one of the country's largest obedience trials I watched a sheltie work the entire Novice class quite unhappily on three legs. It was not a three-legged dog, a subject that the regulations do not cover. It was just so lame that it could not touch the fourth leg to the ground. Outside the ring we were debating how long it would take the judge to excuse the dog. She never did. The most interesting unanswered question that day was why the owner insisted on showing a lame dog.

A variety of reasons can affect a judge's decisions. Some judges consistently give the exhibitor the benefit of the doubt. Some rarely do. At a hot afternoon trial, Tiger and I were the final exhibitors in Utility. Before we showed, several friends confided that our judge was the toughest scoring judge in Southern California and would not score well for any dogs other than poodles and shelties. Encouraged by this cheerful information, I was apprehensive and showed it, which was a mistake. Between the heat and my tension, Tiger decided that he would really rather be somewhere else and proceeded to put on what was actually an amusing performance, although I was in no position to appreciate it just then. It was not that he did not correctly perform all the exercises. He did. But it took him three times as long as usual, while he moved with an air of eloquent disgust and favored me with more offended stares than I had seen in the rest of the year. He worked like a wind-up toy that is running down and about to stop permanently at any moment. He was expressing his opinion of the afternoon's activities. He was also having fun, although his innate honesty would not let him resort to actually failing the exercises. In spite of that, I assumed that his total score would be low enough to be nonqualifying. It would have been had I been judging. But, to my surprise, he did qualify. Then I realized that he was the last dog in a class where only two other dogs had passed. It is one thing to have the reputation of being the toughest judge in the area. There can be a certain pride in that. But it is different to fail almost an entire Utility class. Even that judge did not have the heart to do so.

Tough-scoring judges are not really a problem. Many of them are both fair and knowledgeable. One of my favorite judges is a lady who often draws half the normal size entry for her class because her average score is fairly low. She is also very observant, and as she ticks off those points she will explain to an exhibitor what he is doing to hinder his dog, things that a more casual judge will not even notice. You always leave her ring knowing more than when you entered it.

The Disaster Judge

The real problem to an entrant is the judge who stretches his interpretation of the regulations to the point where he is writing his own rules. The A.K.C. tried to avoid this possibility by including section 5 in the regulations. This section says, "No judge shall require any dog or handler to do anything, nor penalize a dog or handler for failing to do anything, that is not required by these regulations." In other words, judges can reasonably interpret the rules but they are not supposed to add to those rules. This is a thin line and some judges slip over it. This can take two forms. The first is the judge that interprets the rules in an eccentric fashion. You are then showing not only under the A.K.C. rules but also under the judge's rules, which are private. It can be very frustrating.

At an out-of-state trial I went back after class to pick up our Utility scores, only to be surprised to find that neither dog had qualified. They both had been scored zero on the directed retrieve. By that time we had qualified about fifteen times in the class, and as far as I could tell they had qualified that day. For the first time, I asked a trial judge how he happened to arrive at a particular score, and his answer surprised me even further. He had zeroed both dogs in spite of their retrieving the correct gloves because I had neglected to give them a hand signal before sending them out. It was a point of rule interpretation. The rule does say that the handler will give a hand signal. What is not said is whether its omission is to be penalized not at all, or minor points, or thirty points. Since I had never used a signal on this exercise, it is fortunate that we only met one judge who considered the omission worth a thirty-point penalty. You may detect a slight note of discontent in this account, but it is not due to the scoring. I have a little saying that has stood me in good stead from obedience to breed and lure coursing. It is, "All judges are entitled to their opinions, no matter how peculiar I find those opinions."

What irritated me in this instance was that the judge had apparently not bothered to read the *Guidelines for Obedience Judges*. These contain a section that urges the judge to inform the handler, in the ring, should the dog not qualify in an exercise where the nonqualification is not obvious. What the judge had done in this case was fail two consecutive dogs on an obscure point without telling the handler in either case. Had the cause of the failure been revealed with the first dog, the second one would have qualified. This is the sort of thing that creates hard feelings about judges. This particular judge was not having a good day. He had a collection of disappointed exhibitors waiting to ask on what remote technicality they had failed. My favorite was the shepherd owner with a zero score on the directed jumping. During the go away, the handler cues the dog to turn and sit. The dog usually turns when he hears his name and sits when he hears "Sit." In order to give the dog time for the turn there is often a very slight gap between the two words so it becomes "Dog, Sit" instead of "Dogsit." The judge was explaining that the pause between the two words constituted a double command in his opinion and he had failed them for that. It is a good thing the dog was not attack trained. I saw violence gleam in that handler's eye. But it was not needed, because the exhibitors do have the final say. We simply boycotted the judge's next appearance. And, since a large number of utility entrants are also on their clubs' obedience trial committees, this particular judge vanished from the area's shows. The only time that it becomes difficult to exclude an undesired judge is when there is an obedience judge on the obedience committee. The problem here is that some judges are not objective in evaluating other judges. Instead of having judges selected on the basis of their work in the ring, they can be selected or rejected on the basis of personal friendships, personal feuds, trades for future judging assignments, and on criteria that have nothing to do with obtaining the best judge for the trial. However, with sufficient work and perseverance, good judges can be obtained. They far outnumber the occasional reject. There are enough challenges for the exhibitor in coping with himself, the dog, the crowd, and normal rule interpretations without having to worry about the quality of the judging.

The second category of difficult judges contains the hyper-competitors who become judges. The whole sport of obedience has a different meaning to the hyper-competitor than it does to the average exhibitor. Average exhibitors seem to make stable, pleasant judges. The hyper-competitors, on the other hand, move into judging with a group of opinions that do not work well with the A.K.C.'s statement of the purpose of obedience.

It is easy to understand the problem that the hyper-competitor faces when he begins to judge. For years he has been competing against a small group of like souls. He has often scored close to the maximum possible number of points, but then so has his competition. He may even have scored a few 200s. These are the people who are depressed if they score below 195. At some point it occurs to him that, if the judging were only tougher, he might be able to win more often. He has confidence that not only can he teach a dog to do, for instance, a long stand, but that he can teach it not even to blink an eyelash. What he overlooks is that most of his fellow hyper-competitors have sufficient motivation to do the same with their dogs. He then starts to look for ways to maximize the deductions from a dog's score. This can lead to some interesting interpretations of the rules.

I was told by a competitor who will soon be a licensed judge that not enough points were deducted during the long down. I inquired a bit and was told that he thought points should be taken off for any movement by the dog, that is, in order to receive full points, the dog should lie at attention in the sphinx position. All I could ask was "Why?" What would be accomplished except to make the dog less comfortable during the exercise? His reply was that there were too many high-scoring dogs showing and not enough points deducted. This left too many of them at the top of their classes.

Is it possible to have too many good dogs at the top of a class? And what would the totally immobile down do for either the sport or the dog and owner? There is already a move toward this in the hyper-judges, who will deduct points from a dog that sleeps on the long down. They maintain that the dog should remain alert. There is one little problem with this contention. Nowhere in the regulations for this exercise does it say that the dog should remain alert. All that the rules say is that the dog has to remain down in the same place and refrain from barking or whining. The rules do not say that the dog cannot move at all. They only say that the dog is not to move *from the place where it was left*. That leaves the dog considerable freedom for bodily movement. It can roll to its side, shift its weight, sniff the grass, or even eat the grass. No penalty is called for by the regulations for any of these activities, although some judges will score off for them. Such judges are violating Chapter 2, Section 5 of the regulations on No Added Requirements.

The avowed purpose of obedience trials is to demonstrate "the usefulness of the pure bred dog as a companion of man." As a companion, what do we most want of a dog in the down stay? We want him still to be down and where we left him when we return. It is difficult to be concerned over whether he has slept, scratched, or sniffed in the meantime.

What is needed in judging is not increased precision or additional items for which to deduct points but an understanding of the purpose of each exercise and of the sport as a whole. Such understanding should be combined with a knowledge of the rules *as they are written* and the common sense to interpret those rules in the light of the purpose.

A hazard in any judging is that one may be so caught up in looking for minor faults that one may not be able to see the overall quality and balance of a dog in breed or the overall willingness and cooperation shown in an obedience performance. What does the whole dog look like in the ring? Is he a dog you would like to have, and you would like to see more like him? If he wins consistently, you will see more like him in future years. Are we going to have more obedience dogs that are precise but dull and methodical plodders, or do we want dogs that make the sport look fun? That choice depends first on the trainers who take happy dogs into the ring and then on the judges for their evaluations of those dogs.

The Impossible Dog

In the Old West it was possible to make a modest living from the efforts of one really good bucking horse. A man would ride into town with a led horse alongside. He would pass the word around that the horse had never been ridden and that he was willing to back the horse against anyone who thought that he could break it. The suckers would be drawn in like moths to a flame by the challenge of the horse that no one could ride. Well, Old West cowboys are not the only suckers.

When Tiger and Sunny were showing in Novice, a dog of a rare breed was showing in Utility. Jago (pronounced yaw-go) was not qualifying in Utility. When we showed in Open, he was still in Utility, now being shown by a substitute handler, a young man who had responded to the challenge of getting the dog to pass. He had bet the owner that he could succeed where the owner had failed. The young man lost the bet. It was the only time I ever saw a dog urinate on both the scent articles and the jump.

When Tiger and Sunny went to their first Utility match, there was Jago with his owner, dismayed but still practicing. He introduced himself since he felt that people with unusual breeds in Utility should stick together. And he had spent so much time in Utility that he already knew everyone else. We were just roughing out the form of the exercises and ring procedures at that first match, and from our performance he would have been justified in assuming that we would be in

When the section on the Impossible Dog was written, I carefully disguised the identity of the dog in order to save his owner from public exposure. It turned out that his owner wanted the dog identified, so here is the Impossible Dog—American, Mexican, and International Champion Mount Everest Jancsi Jago U.D., P.C.C. He is a komondor, a breed that originated in Hungary. (Photo by Joan Ludwig)

There have been readers who refused to believe that the picture of the Impossible Dog jumping was a photograph of a dog at all. It has been described as a photo of a haystack on a goalpost. For comparison's sake, here is a photograph of a Greyhound making the same jump. In this picture it is possible to recognize minor details like the dog's head, body, and feet. (Photo by Joan Ludwig)

Utility for a good long time. Eight weeks and seven practice matches later we were at our first trial. Four trials later we had three U.D. legs between the two dogs. At this point Jago's owner offered to bet, that he could earn three U.D. legs with Jago before I could finish both Sunny and Tiger. I hate to take a sucker bet, but he insisted. We won, but in a way he won also. Sunny finished at a foggy Pacific Coast Saturday show. The next day we were only showing in breed since it was a hot, inland show. Jago, as always, was in Utility. His owner left his scent articles in the car and went back for them, leaving Jago with a group that contained some of the top trainers in the nation. They had occasionally been intrigued enough by the great hairy problem of Jago to try their hand with him. There was a newcomer in the group who had moved out from the East. For his benefit, talk turned to Jago and his endless nonqualifications. The largest man in the group, a strapping 6'3", two hundred pounder took the dog and the new man with him to the underpass of the adjacent football field. Curious, I followed to watch and had my entire opinion of the dog revised. I had always seen him as a clown, a huge, hairy clown playing to the audience for laughs and frustrating his long-suffering owner by never failing the same way twice.

Until the moment he stepped into the underpass, that is what he was. The handler placed the newcomer in a corner and said with a smile of anticipation, "Watch this!" He then heeled Jago and gave him one firm collar correction. Jago was transformed from a slouchy, surly worker to the epitome of the obedience dog—fast, precise, happy. I was astonished. That single correction on any of my dogs would have totally killed their enthusiasm for the day, but Jago loved it. And then the answer came. As the song puts it, "Different strokes for different folks." Jago was a big, strong, barely domesticated guard dog who admired and respected nothing so much as a demonstration of strength. He had been allowed to become a slob, but if given the strength to bring it out, he had hidden beneath that smelly coat a good working dog. From being accustomed to his failures and indifferent to his performance, I suddenly wanted to see him qualify. The demonstration over, Jago was returned to his unsuspecting owner. The dog promptly reverted to form and worked like his old self. He did not pass. Two months later his owner asked a mutual friend, Sally Perry, and me if we would help him train. At this point he had shown thirty times in Utility over an eighteen-month period without a single qualifying score. He was an irresistible challenge. At that time Sally had four Utility dogs, two sporting, and two working dogs, while I had the two Utility sighthounds. While Jago was stronger than any of us, there was hope that he was not smarter than all three of us.

We started out. Jago and owner would drive up the ninety miles from Los Angeles once a week. First he would go to Sally's, where she would concentrate on mending the relationship between the dog and owner. What the owner needed was confidence that the dog would eventually pass. He also needed to dispel his considerable resentment over all those failures. He needed hope and the ability to love the dog. In addition to the four Utility dogs, Sally has a psychiatrist son, so she went to work on that aspect of the problem. When they were finished I would meet dog and owner at a park to practice, a different park each week. Often a ringwise dog will not act up except at an unfamiliar location, some place that might be a trial. Before showing any dog in a new class, it is valuable to practice in as many locations as possible, to keep the dog from being location-trained and obeying in only one place.

My approach was more pragmatic than Sally's. I did not care if the owner actually loved the dog or not, just as long as he looked as if he loved it. "Come on, smile. I don't care if you hate him, smile at him. Why should he work for you if you don't look happy? All right, relax the face muscles and try it again. If you look at him like you expect him to fail, then he will fail. He will live up to or down to your expectations. That is fine, fake it. There is nothing that says we can't fool him." With repetition, the handler's manner gradually shed its loser's depression. At the same time there was the problem of what to do about Jago's vast repertoire of ring tricks. The more a dog is allowed to misbehave in the ring, the harder it is to ever make him reliable. Jago's thirty tries at Utility had produced an impressive collection of nightmares for the trainer.

The obvious solution was the one I had seen transform him into a good working dog before, namely a strong correction. Here we quickly hit a snag. I had seen Jago corrected by a two-hundred-pound man and he had not objected. But that was eighty pounds more authority than either I or Jago's owner had, and the dog made it perfectly clear that he intended to defend himself against anyone our size, which was pretty close to his size. For our next practice I took along a throw chain that I had been given but never used. They are of no use on a sighthound. But Jago was impressed by it. For two weeks I followed him through the exercises, throw chain in hand, waiting for him to goof off, and then correcting him. He eventually found a counter move. At the first clink of a chain he would drop prone and refuse to budge. He was dropping in the middle of the wrong exercises. That ended the chain's usefulness, but it had been useful. It had given us a means of correcting the dog without having to get within his fight-flight (attack) distance. He was working better except for collapsing at the clink of a chain.

The owner said they had once tried bouncing tennis balls off the dog for corrections. The dog was so heavily coated that he could never have felt a tennis ball's impact, but that reminded me of my hounds' least favorite toy. While they love the figure eight and bone-shaped toys, the hard rubber balls were rejects, just lying ignored in the yard. They may have been reject toys for greyhounds but they made perfect training tools for Jago. For the first time in a correction I heard a ball bounced off his rump produce a slight "Whuff" of surprise, and he decided to heel faster. Since my aim is not all that true, from time to time during the training I would miss the dog, and his owner would give a slight "Whuff" of surprise, but it was worth it. Jago shaped up until he refused to show us any of his old ring tricks. I have seldom seen a happier dog owner than Jago's on the day he qualified in Utility for the first time. Goals that are worked for the longest are often the most rewarding.

Between trials we kept practicing. Showing at alternate trials and practice matches is advisable for any dog working on a U.D. So we took Jago to a practice match with real ring ropes and real ring help. His owner wanted the dog corrected from outside the ring, which I was reluctant to do. At ringside Jago took my favorite greyhound bitch by the throat, shook her, and casually tossed her aside. With a terrified and insulted yelp she bounded into my lap and shivered. She was undamaged except for her pride and her opinion of Jago. It had not done too much for my opinion of him, and I changed my mind about the correction. We had nothing even as impressive as a tennis ball, so I borrowed an apple from lunch and stood at ringside willing the dog to blow it. He looked at the ring, decided that he was on safe territory, and declined to work scent. The judge and help looked a little surprised at having a spectator bash the dog with an apple, but Jago understood. He selected a scent article. Four shows later he finished his U.D. The whole effort had taken twelve weeks and eight trials.

What is the moral of this story? It is not that dogs are trained by bouncing rubber balls or apples off them. What helped Jago would ruin most dogs. We did learn a variety of things from working with Jago though. He made us learn them. First, there is no such thing as a hopeless dog. Unless the owner gives up, the dog will eventually pass. Second, mere practice does not make perfect. Jago had received vast amounts of practice before we intervened. The quality of practice is much more important than its quantity.

Bad practice makes a dog worse.

Good practice makes a dog better.

Only perfect practice makes perfect.

Third, smile and praise the dog, even if it is an act. If it is an act, do it well. The dog reads the handler's expression. If you look angry, why should the dog play your game? Fourth, fit the training to the dog. There are very few dogs with the combination of impervious coat, tough skin, and aggressive personality needed to benefit by the rubber-ball method. On the other hand, Jago's owner now wants a Russian bear dog, so I'll save the throw chain and rubber balls for the future.

Whether the dog is super-aggressive, super-well-adjusted, eager, shy, cooperative, bright, or a little stupid, the training should be what works with that particular dog. The mark of a good trainer is the ability to study each dog and find an appropriate method for it.

The qualities of a good dog are adaptability, resourcefulness, observation, concentration, a spirit of fun, a will to play, curiosity, love for the owner, and respect for the owner.

The qualities of a good trainer are adaptability, resourcefulness, observation, concentration, a spirit of fun, a will to play, curiosity, love for the dog, and respect for the dog.

The Final Word

It is finally time to admit that, in spite of the title, I have not been writing about conventional obedience work. Many readers will have already noticed that. The explanations of the steps taken to induce a dog to perform a particular exercise (what I call the cookbook sections) were given as a guide so that others could learn from my experience. Reading is much quicker than learning by trial and error.

The obedience exercises are simply a framework in which

the dog and owner can learn about themselves and each other. This kind of learning takes place only if there is two-way communication between the pair. Many people do obedience training with the communication all one way, from person to dog. This minimizes the possible rewards of the experience. What I strongly advocate is learning: studying the dogs and ourselves, helping the dogs to learn, while letting them teach us and reveal us to ourselves. The dog is a mirror in which we can see ourselves if we make the effort. While it is a common saying that a dog is an extension of the owner's ego, what is often overlooked is the extent to which the owner's personality acts upon the dog.

While we are busy at work and at daily routines, the dogs have vast amounts of spare time in which to study us and our reactions. Like children, they have the advantage of free time to devote to the study of their favorite subject—us. We have all seen small children who play psychological games with their parents and manipulate the reactions of the distracted adults. This works because the fact that children are small does not make them less intelligent than adults, although it is comforting for the adults to think so. Once the forms of the social behavior patterns are learned—and these are learned very early—a child who is concentrating is easily more than a match for an adult whose attention is divided by outside interests.

Just as children can manipulate parents, dogs can manipulate their owners. What we do in training is pay attention to the dog, to bring to bear on it some of the concentration that it is using on us. In doing this, the dog helps us to learn about subjects that are not generally thought of in connection with dogs, subjects like the phenomena of learning itself, of socialization and habit formation, of communication, of social interaction, and motivation. These are a lot of dry and scholarly words for what makes each of us who he is. So, in the end what one is studying, out on the training field with a friendly dog for help, is oneself.

APPENDIX

Half a Book for Free

There is an incredible number of books on the subject of dog training and obedience. Beware of those books in which the final half of the text is simply a reprint of the American Kennel Club obedience regulations. The regulations are revised yearly, so the version in the book is usually outdated by press time. The A.K.C. will send you a fresh new copy of the obedience regulations. They will also send on request a booklet titled *Guidelines for Obedience Judges*. The trainer will then be able to learn the class rules and find out what the judge is supposed to do to the exhibitor in the ring. Single copies are free. The A.K.C.'s address is 51 Madison Avenue, New York, New York, 10010.

Dog Titles

The American Kennel Club offers nine titles which a dog can earn. When these titles are awarded they are used with the dog's name on the pedigrees of its descendants. The titles, along with a brief description of how each is earned, follow. For more information contact the A.K.C.

The Only Breed Title

Champion (Ch.). This title is earned through competition with others of the dog's breed at dog shows. At each show the best nonchampion of each sex is awarded points toward its

262

championship. These dogs are called the winners dog and winners bitch. The number of points each wins depends on the number of dogs that it defeats. At a single show a dog can earn from zero to five points. The championship is awarded for at least fifteen points. In order to keep a mediocre dog from becoming a Champion through sheer persistence, one point at a time, there is a requirement that the fifteen points include at least two wins, from two judges, that are worth at least three points each. A three, four, or five point win is called a major win. Points earned one or two at a time are called minor points. The competition at dog shows is supposed to determine the best dogs for breeding purposes and is limited to registered, purebred, sexually unaltered dogs and bitches.

The Obedience Titles

Obedience Trial Champion (O.T.Ch). This is the only obedience title that is earned by competition with the other obedience exhibitors. A dog has to have the highest obedience title of Utility Dog before it starts to earn its O.T.Ch. It then competes in the Open B and Utility classes, earning points for class placements.

All of the other obedience titles are earned by having the dog qualify in its class at three obedience trials under three separate judges. Qualification consists of scoring at least 170 of a possible 200 points and by having the dog earn no less than half the points available for each exercise. It is possible to have a total score of more than 170 and still nonqualify by losing most of the points on one exercise. Each qualifying score is called a "leg" on the dog's title. These are the titles and the classes that they are earned in:

Companion Dog (C.D.). The C.D. title is earned in the Novice class. A dog can be shown in Novice only until the owner is notified that the dog has been awarded the Companion Dog title. At every obedience trial two Novice classes are offered, Novice A and Novice B. The difference in the classes is the status of the owner. Dogs in Novice A must be trained and shown by their owner or a member of the owner's immediate family. This person must never have shown a dog to an obedience title before. In Novice B anyone can train or show the dog. The Novice B class is open to any dog that does not yet have a C.D. title.

Companion Dog Excellent (C.D.X.). Before a dog can earn credit towards its C.D.X., it must have earned and been notified of its Companion Dog title by the A.K.C. Impatient owners have trouble waiting for notification, which normally takes six weeks but can take as long as three months. Once your C.D. is confirmed, you can enter the Open A class, which is restricted to dogs that have their C.D. titles but do not yet have a C.D.X. title. Once your dog has earned its C.D.X., you can still show in the Open class but only in the Open B class. The difference between Novice A and Novice B is the qualifications of the owner. The difference between Open A and Open B lies in the qualifications of the dogs. You can enter a non-C.D.X. dog in either Open A or Open B, but in Open A the dog will have less competition and more chances for a class placement. The competition in Open B is much greater since most of the Open B dogs already have their C.D.X. titles.

Utility Dog (U.D.). This is the highest obedience class at the present time. There are proposals for a still more advanced class called the U.D.X., but the American Kennel Club has not accepted the new class yet. A dog must have its C.D.X. before entering Utility. When the class is divided into A and B sections, a dog without a U.D. title can enter either the A or B section, but dogs who have their U.D. title can only enter the B section. Often the Utility class is not divided. If it is just plain Utility, that is the same as Utility B.

The C.D., C.D.X., and U.D. titles are sequential. You have to earn one title before going on to the next one. When used after a dog's name, only the highest title is given since it is understood that he has to have all the preceding titles. Obedience and tracking titles are used after a dog's name, while all of the championship titles—Champion, Field Champion, and Obedience Trial Champion—are used in front of the dog's name. It is possible for a dog's titles to be longer than his name.

Tracking Titles

Tracking Dog (T.D.). The tracking regulations are part of the obedience regulations but tracking titles are not earned at obedience trials. They are earned at tracking tests, and the dog has to qualify only once to earn the title. Before he can even be entered at a tracking test, however, he must be certified by a tracking judge as well enough trained to be eligible to compete. For the T.D. title the dog has to follow a stranger's track that is at least thirty minutes old and has to find an object that was dropped at the end of the track.

Tracking Dog Excellent (T.D.X.). The dog has to follow a track that is more complicated, is older, and is longer than the T.D. track. There is also more than one dropped object to find and he must find all three of them. He must not be mislead by cross tracks.

Hunting Titles

Field Trial Champion (F.Ch). This is a title awarded to hunting dogs for competitive performance in simulated hunting situations. The American Kennel Club awards the title of Field Champion for some breeds of bird dogs and scent hounds. Various other organizations award Field Champion titles for competition at their events. For instance the American Sighthound Field Association holds lure field trials for the breeds of dogs that use visual pursuit and run their game down with sheer speed. These are breeds like the Afghan hound, greyhound, and saluki.

ABBREVIATION KEY

Organizations

A.K.C.	American Kennel Club
A.S.F.A.	American Sighthound Field Association
O.F.A.	Orthopedic Foundation of America

Obedience titles and terms

C.D.	Companion Dog
C.D.,T.D.	Companion Dog, Tracking Dog, a holder of both titles
C.D.X.	Companion Dog Excellent
C.D.X.,T.D.	Companion Dog Excellent, Tracking Dog
U.D.	Utility Dog
U.D.T.	Utility Dog Tracker, holder of both a U.D. and a T.D.
T.D.	Tracking Dog
T.D.X.	Tracking Dog Excellent
O.T. Ch	Obedience Trial Champion
H.I.T.	High in Trial, the highest-scoring dog at an obedience trial

Dog show titles and terms

Ch.	Champion
WB	Winners bitch—the best nonchampion bitch of a breed.
WD	Winners Dog—The best nonchampion dog of a breed

BOW	Best of Winners, either the winners dog or the winners bitch, whichever is best in competition with the other.
BOB	Best of Breed—The best dog of each breed. The champions compete with the winners dog and winners bitch for Best of Breed.
BOS	Best Opposite Sex. If the BOB is won by a dog, then the best opposite sex will be the best bitch. If BOB is won by a bitch, then BOS will be the best dog.
Special	A champion dog competing for Best of Breed
Class Dog or Class Bitch	A nonchampion dog competing in the classes for points toward its championship.
Group Competition	The breeds of dogs are divided into six groups: Sporting, Hounds, Working, Non-Sporting, Toys, and Terriers. The Best of Breed winners within each group compete against each other for group placements.
Group Placer	A dog that has placed second through fourth in group competition
Group Winner	A dog that has won first place in a group. Winning first place in a group allows him to compete with the winners of the other five groups for Best in Show.
B.I.S.	Best In Show

INDEX